Works chosen by Paolo Sprovieri
Catalogue by Maurizio Fagiolo dell'Arco

First published in the United States of America in 1988 by
RIZZOLI INTERNATIONAL PUBLICATIONS, INC.
597 Fifth Avenue, New York, NY 10017

© 1987 by Nuove edizioni Gabriele Mazzotta
Foro Buonaparte 52 - 20121 Milano

ISBN 0-8478-0919-6
LC 87-43275

Printed in Italy

BALLA
The Futurist

by Maurizio Fagiolo dell'Arco

RIZZOLI
NEW YORK

Catalogue Realisation
Coordination: Nadine Bortolotti
Editing: A&P Editing
Translation from Italian: Margaret Kunzle
Paging: Gabriele Miccichè
Cover: G&R Associati
Typesetting: Sedigraf, Milan
Photolithographs: Graphic Studio, S. Giovanni Lupatoto (Verona)
Print: Arti Grafiche Leva A&G, Sesto S. Giovanni (Milan)
Paper: Garda Matt Brillante delle Cartiere del Garda

Photographs
Most of the photographs in this catalogue are by Arte Fotografica, Rome
(Via Tacito 90). A number of colour transparencies are by Ali Elai,
New York, and Peter Schächli, Zurich.
Other photographs are by Pasquale De Antonis, Rome; Alfio Di Bella,
Rome; Alfredo Ferretti, Rome; Gabinetto Fotografico Nazionale, Rome;
Parvum Photo, Milan; Oscar Savio, Rome; Soprintendenza Galleria
Nazionale d'Arte Moderna, Rome; Studio Perotti, Milan; Maurizio
di Puolo, Rome.

The author thanks Luce and Elica Balla, and Giuseppe Sprovieri for their
co-operation. Thanks are also due to Danielle Dutry and Isabella Fischetti.
Documents and information have been provided by: Angelo Calmarini,
Daniela Fonti, Liliana Martano, Giuseppe Sprovieri Jr., Marc Martin-
Malburet, Maurizio Di Puolo, Carla Panicali, Giorgio Chierici, Gina
Severini, Massimo Carpi, Massimo Di Carlo, Alain Tarica, Alessandro Balla.
In New York, thanks go to Lydia Winston-Malbin, Virginia Dortch
Dorazio, Sidney Janis.

Balla in his time - An album of his life and works

AUTOBIOGRAF. BALLA

NEL 500 MI CHIAMAVO LEONARDO

O..... TIZIANO DOPO 4 SECOLI

DI DECADENZA ARTISTICA, SON

RIAPPARSO NEL 900 PER GRIDARE

AI MIEI PLAGIATORI CHE É ORA DI

FINIRLA CON IL PASSATO PERCHÉ

SON CAMBIATI I TEMPI. MI DISSERO

PAZZO: POVERI TONTI !!!!!!!!!!

Ò GIÀ CREATO UNA NUOVA SENSIBILITÀ

NELL'ARTE ~~IMPRESSIONE~~ ESPRESSIONE DEI

TEMPI FUTURI CHE SARANNO

COLORRADIOIRIDESPLENDORIDEAL
LUMINOSISSSSSSSSSIMIIIIIII

FuturBalla

In the Cinquecento my name was Leonardo or... Titian. After four centuries of artistic decadence I reappeared in the twentieth century to cry to my imitators that they must break with the past because times have changed. They called me mad: poor fools!!! I have already created a new sensibility in art, an expression of future times which will be *colorradioiridesplendoridealluminosisssssssssimiiiiii.* *FuturBalla*

This biography in images aims to reconstruct the artist's work together with that of his friends. They were members of a movement, Futurism, which was perhaps the first to propose the integration of "art and life", the declared aim of the Pop Art artists fifty years later.

Balla was very alert to the currents of his time. Often, in keeping with the ideology of Futurism, he even prophesied a new world. So comparative plates illustrate his youthful period and his life with his pupils in Rome, the climate of Socialism and then Futurism, the moment of the war, the utopia of sculpture and of "the Futurist reconstruction of the universe", his contribution to the innovation of stage design and the art of words, his proposal for the cinema and his ideas for new clothing, his inventions in the field of furnishing and brightly coloured household objects, his enthusiasm for "aeropittura" ("aeropainting")... Then there is the story of his exhibitions: from Turin to Rome, from France to Germany, from Switzerland to England, and even in the United States. And his contribution to the international Art Déco scene, his return after 1930 to the "interpretation of naked reality", and finally the postwar years when he was to see his Futurist youth rediscovered.

This album updates and adds new material and analysis to my preceding books: *Futur-Balla* (1965-68, 2nd edition 1970), the Basel catalogue *Balla - A Prophet of the Avant-garde* (1982), and the Vancouver catalogue (1986). Once more I wish to express my gratitude to the artist's daughters, Luce and Elica, for their constant help in my research.

1871-1899. From Turin to Rome

He was born in Turin on 18 July 1871. His father was an industrial chemist by profession, but a lover of art and photography; one of his aunts was a painter. After the death of his father, when Balla was only nine (he had studied music until then), he worked in a lithograph printing shop and later attended evening classes in drawing and (for a few months) the Accademia. His first exhibition was at the Promotrice di Belle Arti in Turin (1891). His early painting was in the local Ottocento tradition, as is evident from the *Self-portrait* of 1894 and a forgotten *View of Turin*. He admired the work of Pellizza da Volpedo and Segantini. In Turin he attended a few lectures by the psychiatrist Cesare Lombroso.

In 1895 he moved to Rome, where he hoped to find work as an architect and also as a decorator, as we see from the sketch for a visiting card. He produced a great many portraits and landscapes; his earliest masterpiece was *March Lights* (*Luci di marzo*), painted the Divisionist technique, exhibited in 1897 at the Promotrice di Belle Arti in Turin. His first shows in Rome were in the rooms of the Amatori e Cultori (1899, 1900).

In a notebook we read: "When the *complete* painter who loves eternal truth in the expression of NATURE is pictorically influenced by her, the currents of transmission are naïve, with no school, method, rule, manner, etc., and virginally sincere. *Born* only because they found those very special senses or nerves scrupulously attuned to artistic creation. He must continue to work this way, otherwise he fabricates fashion. The work of art must be born in the same way as the style of the peoples of the past was born — Goths, Egyptians, Romans etc. Then the unchangeable habits of the present — never past or future — explain the work of art. So when the currents are felt by the verist poet or philosopher, the variety of the pictures will be extraordinary."

Balla (fourth from the left) with his Accademia companions in a photograph by P. Bertieri (on the back: "To our dear friend Balla from his Turin friends 1895").

Self-portrait, 1902. Oil on canvas. Private collection.

View of Turin with the Po, c. 1893. Oil on canvas. Private collection.

Visiting card for the "architect-painter", c. 1899. Watercolour by Balla. Private collection.

Self-portrait, c. 1900. Crayon on paper.
Private collection.

March Lights, 1897. Oil on canvas. Private collection.

Self-caricature, c. 1902. Watercolour on paper.
Private collection.

1900-1904. Divisionism, photography

In September 1900 he went to Paris for the Universal Exhibition, remaining there for seven months. A self-portrait entitled *Self-grimace* (*Autosmorfia*) proclaims his interest in "dynamic states of mind". A *Self-portrait*, after his return to Italy, confirms and clarifies his use of the Divisionist technique, closer to Pellizza da Volpedo's light than to French Pointillism. He began to show regularly: at the Amatori e Cultori in Rome (1902, 1903, 1904), at the Turin Quadriennial (1902, the same year as Pellizza da Volpedo exhibited *The Fourth · Estate*), and at the Venice Biennial (1903). In 1904 he married Elisa Marcucci and went to live with her in a deconsecrated monastery in the Parioli, at that time an outlying district of Rome (it remained his studio up to 1926).

The masterpiece of the period is *Bankruptcy* (*Fallimento*), in which the bottom half of a shop closed up for bankruptcy is analyzed in every detail, more real than life. Thirty years later Balla had himself photographed in front of this painting to demonstrate his intention of absolute truth. In other paintings he focusses on the image in a way that suggests photography. In the portrait of his mother — very bold in its large format — he experiments with an "enlargement", in the portrait of his wife he is "focussing", while in the self-portrait entitled *Self-shoulder* (*Autospalla*) he tries out a "detail".

In an autobiographical note he wrote: "'Art 1st period: personal, verist, objective — analysis of daily life — solution Divisionist explorations (lights, environments — psyche, objects, people)".

There is a misunderstanding in modern historiography about this that should be set straight. The point is not that Balla came close to photography, passively adopting its procedures and its tricks. The truth is that the artist's mentality was "photographic" — he did not need to mimic another technique since his own eye saw "objectively".

Self-grimace, 1900. Crayon on paper. Private collection.

Self-portrait, c. 1894. Oil on paste-board. Rome, Banca d'Italia.

The artist photographed in front of the painting *Bankruptcy* (1902), held by his daughter Luce, in a photograph taken by Ambassador Cosmelli c. 1927.

The Artist's Wife Elisa, c. 1905. Crayon on paper. Private collection.

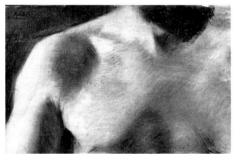

Self-shoulder. Oil on canvas. Private collection.

Portrait of the Artist's Mother, 1901. Crayon on paper. Private collection.

11

1901-1905. Family and pupils

Balla's attention as an artist was always turned to his family — his mother, his fiancée and then wife, Elisa, himself, and later his daughters. Particularly fine is the life-size portrait of his wife painted in 1904: Elisa (pregnant with the daughter they were to call Luce, "Light"), is set against the open door on the right from which light floods in, in a sort of secular Annunciation.

A separate chapter in Balla's life was his relationship with his students. Severini wrote later: "Boccioni, who had a flair for recognizing people of merit, discovered Balla, who had just come back from Paris." And, "In a general environment of vulgarity, banality and mediocrity, the severe figure of Balla stood out. Following his example and as a reaction to this sort of environment, both Boccioni's and my work became more aggressive and violent — we had both made progress."

Another painter who frequented Balla's studio was Mario Sironi, who subsequently followed other paths. Their youthful works owe a great deal to Balla. Umberto Boccioni was influenced by his iconography and by his dynamic brushwork (a revised Divisionism). Gino Severini, in a self-portrait published in *Avanti della Domenica*, was inspired by the master's photographic "cutting", while Sironi explored a similar poetic vision, combining intimism with social concern.

Self-portrait, c. 1909. Enamel on paste-board. Private collection.

Elisa in the Doorway, 1904. Crayons, tempera and charcoal on paper. Private collection.

A party in his studio in honour of American friends. Balla is at the centre beside the flag; at the head of the table on the right is Elisa with their daughter Luce. Among the paintings visible: *The Beggar, Elisa in the Doorway, The Madwoman of Via Parioli, The New Plane*.

Gino Severini in a self-portrait (1905), published in *Avanti della Domenica*.

Umberto Boccioni in a self-portrait of 1907.

Mario Sironi in a self-portrait of 1908.

Gino Severini, *The Street Light at Porta Pinciana*, 1903.

Umberto Boccioni, *My Mother*, 1907.

Mario Sironi, *The Mother Sewing,* 1905.

Humanitarian Socialism

Balla took an active part in the new social movements, being influenced by Pellizza da Volpedo (*The Fourth Estate*) and Tolstoy's preaching. His paintings dedicated to work are religious in tone, as can be seen in *The Working Man's Day* (*La giornata dell'operaio*), where spatial divisions mark different moments of a proletarian life. His paintings dedicated to social symbols, such as *The Madwoman* (*La pazza*), are a denunciation of the isolation produced by false progress. Balla provided cover illustrations (with Boccioni and Severini) for the left-wing paper *Avanti della Domenica*, he was friendly with Giovanni Cena and his companion Sibilla Aleramo, and met Maxim Gorky; Severini and Boccioni read Marx, Bakunin and Labriola.

In Rome the political climate had changed. The mayor was Ernesto Nathan, a Freemason and anticleric, who in the few years of his office brought a new atmosphere to the city (Balla painted a fine portrait of him).

Painting light again for its symbolical meaning, he had Pellizza da Volpedo's solemn manifesto before his eyes, where the humanitarian ideal of the "sun of the future" is first of all a brilliant pictorial experiment.

He made a significant contribution to the pavilion designed by Giovanni Cena and his brother-in-law Marcucci for the Universal Exhibition in Rome in 1911, which displayed the results of the education campaign among the migrant peasants of the Roman Campagna and Pontine marshes. In the main hall hung ten paintings by Balla dedicated to peasant life, arranged around a portrait of Tolstoy. This was the concrete result of Balla's social commitment: an authentic immersion in the proletarian world, a "saison à l'enfer" at the gates of Rome with the missionary urge of a Van Gogh. It may be recalled that the Pointillists were inspired by similar humanitarian ideals — Seurat was the friend of anarchists and socialists and a painter of working people, Signac had painted the utopian picture *At the Time of Harmony*.

Giuseppe Pellizza da Volpedo, *The Fourth Estate*, 1898-1901.

Giuseppe Pellizza da Volpedo, *The Rising Sun*, 1904.

Portrait of Tolstoy, 1910. Oil on canvas. Private collection.

Portrait of Ernesto Nathan, 1910. Oil on canvas. Galleria Comunale d'Arte Moderna, Rome.

The Working Man's Day, 1904. Triptych, oil on paper. Private collection.

The Madwoman on the Balcony in Via Paisiello, 1905. Oil on canvas. Private collection.

1909-1911. Futurism

It was in Balla's studio that Boccioni and Severini worked and became converted to "Modernism". In 1910 they invited him to sign the *Manifesto of Futurist Painting*. The movement's manifesto had been proclaimed the previous year by Filippo Tommaso Marinetti in *Le Figaro* and the rallies of the future were already depicted in the magazine *Poesia*.

In 1912 the young Futurists went to Paris for a show that aroused wide interest. With a painting like *Street Light* (*Lampada ad arco*) (listed in the Paris catalogue but not shown), Balla proposed a modernist subject matter while remaining basically faithful to his concern with objective analysis.

Boccioni, who with his *States of Mind* (*Stati d'animo*) seemed the member of the group most projected into the future, did not fail to criticize his ex-teacher. Balla's painting is contemporary with *Let's Kill Moonlight!*, one of the hundred manifestos with which Marinetti established the avant-garde.

In the meantime Balla continued to exhibit his "objective verist" works. In 1909 he was present at the Paris Salon d'Automne with the four paintings "Dei viventi" ("On Living Beings") and three other canvases (he showed in the same room as Previati). Later that year he sent seven large works — which have recently resurfaced — to the Odessa and St Petersburg exhibitions. In 1910, in Rome, he exhibited the painting called *Waving* (*Salutando*), in which objectivity is combined with his new Futurist interests, movement and light.

Futurist Parade (caricature by Manca) from F.T. Marinetti's magazine *Poesia*, 1909.

The exhibition in Paris, 1912. Boccioni and Marinetti beside Boccioni's canvas *Laughter*.

16

Street Light, 1909. Oil on canvas. The Museum of Modern Art, New York.

Marinetti in a "synthetic portrait" by Balla. China ink on paper. Private collection.

F. T. MARINETTI

Uccidiamo il chiaro di luna!

EDIZIONI FUTURISTE
DI "POESIA,,
MILANO - Via Senato, 2
1911

The frontispiece of the pamphlet *Let's Kill Moonlight!*, 1911.

1912. Analysis of movement

Over a few months — first in Tuscany, then in Rome and finally in Düsseldorf where he was called to decorate a house — Balla started a new line of exploration. In *Dynamism of a Dog on a Leash* (*Dinamismo di un cane al guinzaglio*) movement is created by a visible breaking-down into stages. One of Bragaglia's first experiments in "photodynamism" was dedicated to Balla and this painting. He continued his analytical study with the breaking-down of the steps of the *Girl Running on a Balcony* (*Bambina che corre sul balcone*). His experimental cycles, Leonardesque in feeling, started: the series of "Swifts", first caught in light and then in dynamic succession, and the "Speeding Cars". Balla begins with an objective analysis in his notebook pages and goes on to achieve a sort of synthesis of speed. Defined by the Futurist manifesto as "more beautiful than the Victory of Samothrace", the automobile became the symbol of the "victory" over the difficulties of pictorial representation.

In the meantime Balla participated in Futurist events. In 1911 he was present at the lecture given by Boccioni at the Circolo Artistico in Rome (which was followed by a riot at the Café Aragno), and at the talk and exhibition of "photodynamics" by his friend Anton Giulio Bragaglia at the Libreria Mantegazza. In 1914 he took part in the event at the Costanzi Theatre, when Papini pronounced his impassioned speech against Rome and an exhibition was organized in the foyer with some fifty works. Balla exhibited *Dynamism of a Dog on a Leash*, *Bow Rhythms* (*Ritmi di archetto*), *Street Light*, *Girl Running on a Balcony* (entitled *Girl Multiplied Balcony - Bambina moltiplicata balcone*), and an *Iridescent Penetration* (*Penetrazione iridescente*).

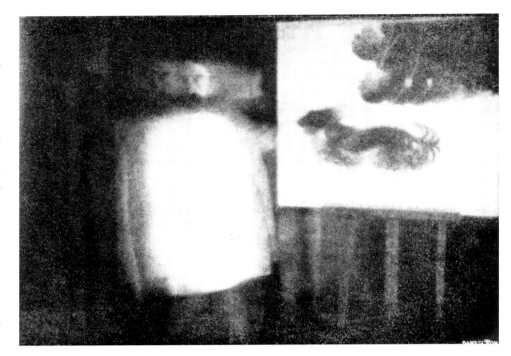

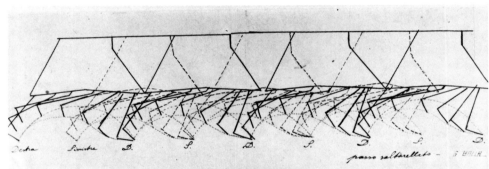

A "fotodinamica" by Anton Giulio Bragaglia showing Balla in front of the painting *Dynamism of a Dog on a Leash* (1912, now in The Albright-Knox Art Gallery, Buffalo).

Skipping Step, for *Girl Running on a Balcony*, 1912. Inks on paper. Private collection.

Rhythms of the Violinist, 1912. Oil on canvas. The Tate Gallery, London (on loan, Eric Estorick collection).

Swifts' Flight, 1913. Oil on canvas. Private collection.

Two sketches for cars (from his notebooks). Pencil on paper. Casa Balla.

Lines of Direction + Dynamic Succession + Swifts' Flight, 1913. Oil on canvas. The Museum of Modern Art, New York.

Speeding Car, 1912. Oil on wood. The Museum of Modern Art, New York.

1912-1914. Analysis of light

In December 1912 Balla was in Düsseldorf. In the canvas *Window in Düsseldorf* he focusses on the misty light of the North, the reflection of the window and the symbol of vision, binoculars. Now he began to work on paintings of luminous triangles in rainbow colours, which he immediately called "Iridescent Interpenetrations". It should be noted how the breaking-down of light into triangular forms proceeds parallel with the equally geometrical breaking-down of the girl's steps. In a letter to his family he communicated his intentions: experimental research (he talks about "testing and re-testing"), to be scientific but also joyful (he mentions "observation from life" and "delight") and his aim to achieve simplicity. In 1914 he adapted the iridescent triangle motif for his poster for the "Secession" exhibition and developed it in a series of paintings that are among the first consciously abstract works in Europe.

His letters to his family from Düsseldorf describe his work and new experimentation: "Electric light with all sorts of phosphorescent and fantastic effects. [...] I've finished four pictures for the drawing room [...] and now I'm also finishing a study of the husband's hand playing the violin, but moving in different positions, with the constant passage of the bow over these movements. The work is something absolutely new and the lady is enchanted with it" (18 November).

"My very dear ones. First of all just enjoy this little spectrum because I'm positive you'll like it; it's the result of endless testing and re-testing and finally achieves its aim of delighting through simplicity. This work will produce other changes in my painting and through observation from life the spectrum will reveal and convey innumerable colour sensations" (5 December).

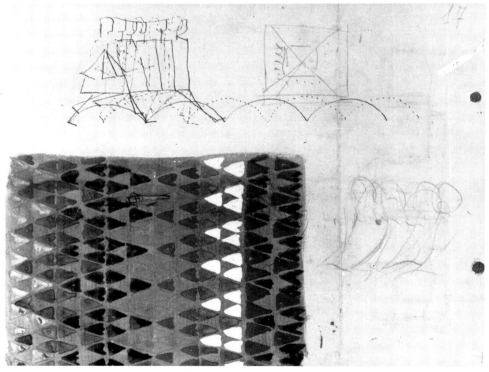

Letter to his family announcing the beginning of his work on "Iridescent Interpenetrations", 1912.

In a photograph of 1913, wearing the tie with the "Iridescent Interpenetrations" motif.

Notebook page with the two contemporary studies of a "Girl's Step" and "Iridescent Interpenetrations".

Window in Düsseldorf with Binoculars, 1912 c. Oil on wood. Private collection.

Notebook page with the "Iridescent Interpenetrations" motif, adapted as a poster for the Rome Secession exhibition, 1913.

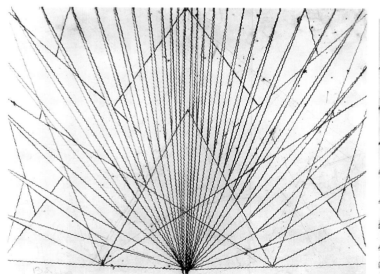

Radial Iridescent Interpenetration - Prismatic Vibrations, c. 1913. Coloured inks on paper. Private collection.

Study for the Interpenetration of Planes, c. 1913. Pencil on paper. Private collection.

1913-1914. The Futurist impulse

Having entered the Futurist movement on tiptoe, Balla succeeded in becoming a guiding star for his ex-pupils, Boccioni and Severini. In April 1913, to close symbolically with his past, he put his earlier paintings up for auction, as we read in a handbill — a Pirandellian suicide.

In Balla's studio there were theatrical performances in a brilliantly coloured, vital atmosphere, while the artist even found himself reciting during *soirées* at Giuseppe Sprovieri's Galleria Futurista. After the long period of private experimentation, he returned to the outside world with shows of his latest works, magazine covers, controversies and debates. Even Boccioni, who had mistrusted Balla's analytical exploration, appreciated his "very rapid evolution".

Now his paintings appeared frequently before the public. In 1913 he was on the committee of the Rome Secession (the French school also participated, with the Impressionists, Matisse and Rodin) and according to Giuseppe Sprovieri, designed a decoration of "Iridescent Interpenetrations" in a corridor of the Palazzo delle Esposizioni. At the Futurist exhibition in Rotterdam in June he showed his four paintings of movement. *Rhythms of the Violinist* and *Dynamism of a Dog on a Leash* (exhibited as *A Moving Leash*, *Un guinzaglio in movimento*) were also shown at the *Der Sturm* exhibition (Berlin, September). In November four paintings dedicated to the speed of cars were included in the *Lacerba* exhibition in Florence (two were reproduced the following year in Soffici's *Cubismo e futurismo*).

Important among his 1914 showings was the room with 28 canvases at the Amatori e Cultori in Rome (an *Iridescent Interpenetration* was included), his participation in the "Esposizione di pittura futurista" at Sprovieri's gallery, and the London Futurist exhibition (four paintings of "Speeding Cars").

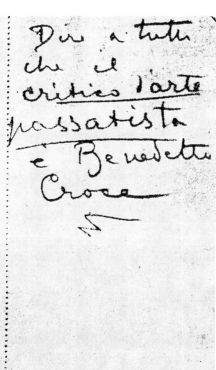

Balla in his studio (1918) with a young American artist, holding a large fist used for a Futurist event.

Front page

Self-state of Mind, from the catalogue of the exhibition at the Sala Angelelli, Rome, December 1915.

Announcement by Balla for the sale of his "passéist paintings" at the Galleria Giosi, Rome, 1913.

Sketch by Balla for the magazine *Dinamo*, 1913. China ink on paper. Private collection.

Sketch made by Severini in 1913 for a Galleria Sprovieri exhibition (1914).

A written page from Balla's notebook reflecting the atmosphere of the period: "Tell everybody that the passéist art critic is Benedetto Croce."

GALLERIA PERMANENTE FUTURISTA
Direttore: G. SPROVIERI
1ª ESPOSIZIONE FUTURISTA NAPOLETANA
in VIA DEI MILLE, 16 (Palazzo Spinelli)

Domenica 17 Maggio alle ore 15
il pittore futurista

BALLA

stimolerà gli artisti napoletani verso nuove forme d'arte col
DINAMISMO PLASTICO

Il poeta futurista

CANGIULLO

declamerà
SERATA IN ONORE D' YVONNE
parole in libertà con accompagnamento orchestrale onomatopeico di

BALLA

MARINETTI

telefonerà da Londra al pubblico dell' Esposizione le sue nuove parole in libertà.
BIGLIETTO D' INGRESSO L. 1.

L'ESPOSIZIONE È APERTA ogni giorno fino al 10 giugno, dalle ore 10 alle 19.

The members of the Futurist group, in a letter from Balla to Marinetti.

Handbill for a performance by Balla at the Galleria Sprovieri, Naples, 1914.

1913-1917. Synthesis of movement

After the extremes of analysis, Balla reached his own form of synthesis. From the immobile car he passed to a study of the movement of wheels, fusing environmental factors such as light and sound. At this stage he worked out the "Line of Speed". This line, schematic and abstract (Balla called it "the fundamental basis of my thought-forms") was henceforth to be at the centre of his work. He brought it into space with his first thread-like sculptures and combined it with other sensations. In the same period Boccioni was doing his most decidedly Futurist work, while Severini in a one-man show in London exhibited his research on synthetic dynamism.

In Balla's case, the research ended not on the easel but on the stage, with the construction of coloured forms animated solely by light for *Feu d'artifice*, put on in Rome in 1917 by Diaghilev's Ballets Russes. Considerable space was dedicated to the performance in *Sic*, the magazine edited by Pierre Albert-Birot in Paris (May 1917): "The sculptural set designed for Stravinsky's *Feu d'artifice* by the Futurist painter Balla constitutes the great novelty of the Rome performances, not so much for the work in itself, perhaps, as for the new questions it raises. [...] By introducing a quite unexpected play of light and colour on plastic forms, Balla's design upsets the normal standard of stage settings. Avant-garde artists now have an immense field of research before them, and those familiar with their intense vitality and the creative resources of their talent can hardly doubt that very soon there will be further and better attempts in this direction. But whatever happens, Balla will remain the artist who first traced out this path, and this fact on its own is enough to consecrate his very real value as an artist and innovator."

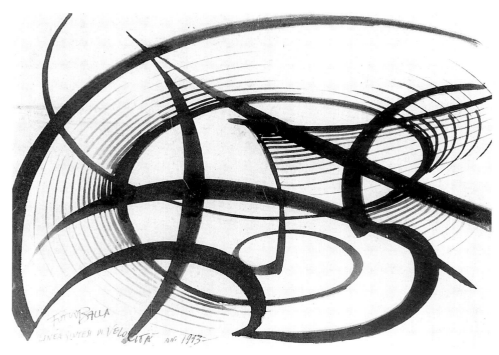

Synthesis of the Line of Speed, 1913. China ink on paper. The Museum of Modern Art, Toronto.

Line of Speed, 1913. Tempera on paper. Private collection.

Umberto Boccioni with his large palette in front of the painting *Matter*.

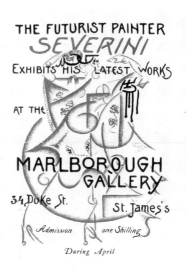

Gino Severini's latest paintings on show in London, April 1913.

Sketch for *Feu d'artifice*, staged by Diaghilev's Ballets Russes at the Costanzi Theatre in Rome, April 1917 (from *L'Italia Futurista*, August 1917).

1913-1914. "Futurist Painting Sculpture"

In 1913 Balla was in Milan, where he was photographed together with Boccioni's mother beside one of his ex-pupil's extraordinary sculptures. Boccioni was finishing his book *Pittura Scultura Futuriste,* published in February 1914. Balla complimented him on this bible of the movement, "a wonderful book after centuries of corpse-art." In a postcard he also saluted Carrà's "free-word" book *Guerrapittura* with enthusiasm. But the figure he looked to remained Marinetti. Balla recognized his role as leader and his ability to create agit-prop for culture. In those two years Balla also guided fresh talents into the movement: the painters Depero and Prampolini, and the many-sided Francesco Cangiullo. Boccioni's message was almost exhausted. The leadership of the movement — Severini was working in Paris — seemed to pass to Balla and its centre seemed to shift from Milan to Rome, where in December 1913 Giuseppe Sprovieri opened his Galleria Futurista.

The first exhibition was dedicated to Boccioni's sculpture. While the show was on, evenings of poetry alternated with music (Balilla Pratella and Russolo's *intonarumori,* "noise-tuners"). In February 1914 the "Esposizione di pittura futurista" opened, where Balla showed beside Boccioni, Carrà, Russolo, Severini and Soffici. During the exhibition there was a succession of *soirées* dedicated to poetry and "words in freedom". Balla took part in some of the events, which could be defined as "happenings". In April the "Esposizione libera futurista internazionale" was inaugurated. In May a branch of the gallery opened in Naples. Balla participated actively in the exhibitions and events. A few months later, the lively period ended with Sprovieri's departure for the war front (on this period, see M. Fagiolo, *Esposizione di pittura futurista*, Marsilio, Venezia, 1986).

Balla in Milan in Boccioni's studio, beside the artist, his mother, and his sculpture *Synthesis of Human Dynamism*, 1913.

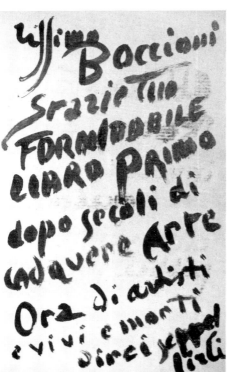

BOCCIONI
FUTURISTA

PITTURA SCULTURA FUTURISTE

(DINAMISMO PLASTICO)

CON 51 RIPRODUZIONI
QUADRI SCULTURE
DI BOCCIONI - CARRÀ
RUSSOLO - BALLA
SEVERINI - SOFFICI

EDIZIONI FUTURISTE
DI "POESIA"
MILANO - CORSO VENEZIA, 61
1914

The frontispiece of Boccioni's book *Futurist Painting-Sculpture*, February 1914.

Letter from Balla to Boccioni with compliments on his "amazing book".

Letter from Balla to Boccioni, 7 February 1914.

A caricature referring to Marinetti's "triumphs" in Milan and Moscow, 1914.

Giuseppe Sprovieri, the twenty-three year old director of the Galleria Futurista in Rome, 1913.

Postcard from Balla to Carrà complimenting him on his book *Guerrapittura*.

1915. Risks of war

The Futurists saw war as "the world's great cleanser", and "interventionism" (support for Italian participation) was for Balla not only a moral position but also a vivid summing-up of his youthful enthusiasm.

To the Futurists, as Marinetti's manifesto makes clear, the war was a chance to break with the old "passéist" world. The nations at war were defined as "poet-peoples" and ultimately the whole thing was seen as a colossal aesthetic operation (although Marinetti, Boccioni and Sant'Elia put theory into practice and were among the first to leave for the front as volunteers).

Balla's paintings were greatly appreciated by Boccioni, who for his part saw the war as a new possibility for breaking down the image (retaining however a connection to his figurative past). Severini chose a more symbolic and at the same time plastic interpretation. An unexpected combination or "free-word synthesis" with typography was made by Carrà in his book *Guerrapittura*.

During 1915 Balla was twice involved with the police: in February at Montecitorio, outside Parliament, with Marinetti, Cangiullo and others, and in April in Piazza di Trevi with Marinetti, Depero, Mussolini, Corra and Settimelli. The first paintings dedicated to interventionist rallies appeared in the "Esposizione Fu Balla, e Balla Futurista", held at the Sala Angelelli in December. The whole series was subsequently shown at the Casa d'Arte Bragaglia in October 1918.

"Free-word synthesis" on the war, signed by Marinetti, Boccioni, Carrà, Russolo and Piatti, 20 September 1914.

The Futurists at the front, 1915. From the left: Marinetti, Sant'Elia, Russolo, Boccioni, Sironi.

DIZIONI FUTURISTE
DI "POESIA„
Corso Venezia, 61 - MILANO
1915

War, 1915. Collage. Banco di Roma collection.

The frontispiece of Carrà's book, 1915.

Gino Severini, *Synthèse plastique de l'idée guerre*, 1915.
Umberto Boccioni, *Charge of the Lancers*, 1915.

Balla felt a positively physical need to extend his interest from the canvas to the environment. His idea of a "Futurist reconstruction of the universe" (theorized in a manifesto of 1915) was put into practice with increasingly important experiments in decoration. In his manifesto on clothes (ideologically revamped by Marinetti) Balla applied his idea of a lively, joyous art to the world around him. Helped by his daughter Luce, he began to make clothes to be worn by himself and his friends. In his studio Balla appeared like the prophet of a brightly coloured transformation of the living environment (the paper *Roma Futurista* published an announcement recommending readers to visit "Balla's Futurist house"). He designed furniture for himself and a number of friends and made objects for the few patrons of the time. He tried to bring into the home the dynamic idea behind his painting.

It is symptomatic that this "overall" attitude to creativity arose following his visit to Düsseldorf: only the Secession climate could have made Balla aware of the possibility of abolishing all the barriers between "major" and "minor" arts. His most important achievement was the furniture for Casa Balla (1918-20); today there remain a large assembled piece and the table, chairs, bench and sofa, all in yellow and green. To decorate a living space became this craftsman-painter's fixed aspiration. Before reconstructing the universe he set about enlivening his own chrysalis.

In the manifesto *Il futurismo italiano nel 1921*, among the achievements listed are "Futurist decorative art by Balla (ceramics, screens, lamps etc.), workshop in Rome; *Bal Tik Tak*, a large hall for night dancing in Rome, futuristically decorated by Balla". His interest in household objects was paralleled by Metaphysical painting and foreshadowed Dada. Balla wrote that a glittering shop was more beautiful than an exhibition of paintings, an electric iron more valuable than a sculpture and a typewriter more important than pretentious architecture.

IL VESTITO ANTINEUTRALE
Manifesto futurista

Glorifichiamo la guerra, sola igiene del mondo.
MARINETTI.
(1° Manifesto del Futurismo - 20 Febbraio 1909)

Viva Asinari di Bernezzo!
MARINETTI.
(1ª Serata futurista - Teatro Lirico, Milano, Febbraio 1910)

L'umanità si vestì sempre di **quiete**, di **paura**, di **cautela** o d'**indecisione**, portò sempre il lutto, o il piviale, o il mantello. Il corpo dell'uomo fu sempre diminuito da sfumature e da tinte **neutre**, avvilito dal nero, soffocato da cinture, imprigionato da panneggiamenti.

Fino ad oggi gli uomini usarono abiti di colori e forme statiche, cioè drappeggiati, solenni, gravi, incomodi e sacerdotali. Erano espressioni di timidezza, di malinconia e di **schiavitù**, negazione della vita muscolare, che soffocava in un passatismo anti-igienico di stoffe troppo pesanti e di mezze tinte tediose, effeminate o decadenti. Tonalità e ritmi di **pace desolante**, funeraria e deprimente.

OGGI vogliamo abolire:

1. — Tutte le tinte **neutre**, « carine », sbiadite, *fantasia*, semioscure e umilianti.

2. — Tutte le tinte e le foggie pedanti, professorali e teutoniche. I disegni a righe, a quadretti, a **puntini diplomatici.**

3. — I vestiti da lutto, nemmeno adatti per i becchini. Le morti eroiche non devono essere compiante, ma ricordate con vestiti rossi.

4. — L'equilibrio **mediocrista**, il cosidetto buon gusto e la cosidetta armonia di tinte e di forme, che frenano gli entusiasmi e rallentano il passo.

5. — La simmetria nel taglio, le linee **statiche**, che stancano, deprimono, contristano, legano i muscoli; l'uniformità di goffi risvolti e tutte le cincischiature. I bottoni inutili. I colletti e i polsini inamidati.

Noi futuristi vogliamo liberare la nostra razza da ogni **neutralità**, dall'indecisione paurosa e quietista, dal pessimismo negatore e dall'inerzia

Vestito bianco - rosso - verde
portato dal parolibero futurista Cangiullo, nelle dimostrazioni dei Futuristi contro i professori tedescofili e neutralisti dell'Università di Roma (11-12 Dicembre 1914).

Manifesto dedicated to clothing, 11 September 1914 (a first edition appeared in France on 20 May of the same year; the original manuscript still exists).

Balla in his studio around 1930 in a Futurist suit. In the background, Futurist art: a tapestry, items of furniture, flowers, objects.

Design by Balla for a Futurist interior, 1918. Tempera on paper. Private collection.

Synthesis by Balla of Futurist objects. From the periodical *Rassegna dell'Arte e del Lavoro*, Rome, 25 March 1922.

Future-reality, 1917. Tempera on paper. Private collection.

1914-1915. Constructivist sculpture

In his extraordinary manifesto on the "reconstruction of the universe" (where with Depero he signed himself "Futurist abstractionist"), Balla published three "Plastic Ensembles" made in the winter of 1914. Here he described the multiple possibilities of movement, transparency and sound applied to sculpture, and to what was to be the new sculpture. The basic idea, just as that of the Russians, was not to destroy but to create (however the manifesto for Constructivism signed by Gabo and Pevsner appeared only in 1920). Balla stubbornly built the structures of the future with new, perishable materials — cardboard, wire, celluloid, woollen yarn, foil, mirrors. The sculpture *Force-lines of Boccioni's Fist* (*Linee di forza del pugno di Boccioni*) was initially also made of cardboard; it transformed Boccioni's idea of the body into an abstract form.

La marchesa Casati (owned by Marinetti), published on the cover of *Il Mondo*, was an object of wood and cardboard. It was also a dynamic sculpture because the spectator was invited to shift the lower part, corresponding to the heart, to see the movement of the eyes.

In the 1915 manifesto we read: "Balla began by studying the speed of automobiles and discovered their laws and essential force-lines. After more than twenty paintings of this sort he understood that the single plane of the canvas did not allow him to reproduce the dynamic volume of speed in depth. Balla felt the need to build the first dynamic plastic ensemble using wire, cardboard, fabrics, tissue-paper, etc.

"1. ABSTRACT. 2. DYNAMIC. Relative motion (cinematograph) + absolute motion. 3. EXTREMELY TRANSPARENT. Because of the speed and volatility of the plastic ensemble, which must appear and disappear, very very light and impalpable. 4. HIGHLY COLOURED - BRIGHTLY LIT (by means of light-bulbs placed inside). 5. AUTONOMOUS, i.e. resembling only itself. 6. TRANSFORMABLE. 7. DRAMATIC. 8. VOLATILE. 9. ODOROUS. 10. NOISY. Plastic noisiness adapted to the plastic expression. 11. EXPLOSIVE. Simultaneous appearance and disappearance in bursts."

Force-lines of Boccioni's Fist (*no. 1*), 1915.

RICOSTRUZIONE FUTURISTA DELL'UNIVERSO

Leggete LA BALZA GIORNALE FUTURISTA MESSINA

Col Manifesto tecnico della Pittura futurista e colla prefazione al Catalogo dell' Esposizione futurista di Parigi (firmati Boccioni, Carrà, Russolo, Balla, Severini), col Manifesto della Scultura futurista (firmato Boccioni), col Manifesto La Pittura dei suoni rumori e odori (firmato Carrà), col volume *Pittura e scultura futuriste*, di Boccioni, e col volume *Guerrapittura*, di Carrà, il futurismo pittorico si è svolto, in 6 anni, quale superamento e solidificazione dell'impressionismo, dinamismo plastico e plasmazione dell'atmosfera, compenetrazione di piani e stati d'animo. La valutazione lirica dell'universo, mediante le Parole in libertà di Marinetti, e l'Arte dei Rumori di Russolo, si fondono col dinamismo plastico per dare l'espressione dinamica, simultanea, plastica, rumoristica della vibrazione universale.

Noi futuristi, Balla e Depero, vogliamo realizzare questa fusione totale per ricostruire l'universo rallegrandolo, cioè ricreandolo integralmente. Daremo scheletro e carne all'invisibile, all'impalpabile, all'imponderabile, all'impercettibile. Troveremo degli equivalenti astratti di tutte le forme e di tutti gli elementi dell'universo, poi li combineremo insieme, secondo i capricci della nostra ispirazione, per formare dei complessi plastici che metteremo in moto.

Balla cominciò collo studiare la velocità delle automobili, ne scoprì le leggi e le linee-forze essenziali. Dopo più di 20 quadri sulla medesima ricerca, comprese che il piano unico della tela non permetteva di dare in profondità il volume dinamico della velocità. Balla sentì la necessità di costruire con fili di ferro, piani di cartone, stoffe e carte veline, ecc., il primo complesso plastico dinamico.

1. Astratto. — 2. Dinamico. Moto relativo (cinematografo) + moto assoluto. — **3. Trasparentissimo.** Per la velocità e per la volatilità del complesso plastico, che deve apparire e scomparire, leggerissimo e impalpabile. — **4. Coloratissimo e Luminosissimo** (mediante lampade interne). — **5. Autonomo,** cioè somigliante solo a sè stesso. — **6. Trasformabile. — 7. Drammatico. — 8. Volatile. — 9. Odoroso. — 10. Rumoreggiante.** Rumorismo plastico simultaneo coll'espressione plastica. — **11. Scoppiante,** apparizione e scomparsa simultanee a scoppi.

Il parolibero Marinetti, al quale noi mostrammo i nostri primi complessi plastici ci disse con entusiasmo: « L'arte, prima di noi, fu ricordo, rievocazione angosciosa di un Oggetto perduto « (felicità, amore, paesaggio) perciò nostalgia, statica, dolore, lontananza. Col Futurismo invece, l'arte « diventa arte-azione, cioè volontà, ottimismo, aggressione, possesso, penetrazione, gioia, realtà brutale nell'arte (Es.: onomatopee. — Es.: intonarumori = motori), splendore geometrico delle forze, « proiezione in avanti. Dunque l'arte diventa Presenza, nuovo Oggetto, nuova realtà creata cogli « elementi astratti dell'universo. Le mani dell'artista passatista soffrivano per l'Oggetto perduto; « le nostre mani spasimavano per un nuovo Oggetto da creare. Ecco perchè il nuovo Oggetto « (complesso plastico) appare miracolosamente fra le vostre. »

La costruzione materiale del complesso plastico

MEZZI NECESSARI: Fili metallici, di cotone, lana, seta, d'ogni spessore, colorati. Vetri colorati, carteveline, celluloidi, reti metalliche, trasparenti d'ogni genere, coloratissimi. tessuti,

BALLA

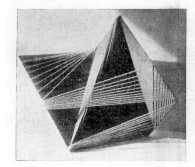

N. 3. Complesso plastico colorato di linee-forze
(Cartone, lana, filo rosso, filo giallo)

DEPERO

N. 5. Complesso plastico colorato motorumorista simultaneo di scomposizione a strati

DEPERO

N. 4. Complesso plastico colorato
(Latte e carte colorate)

DEPERO

N. 6. Complesso plastico colorato motorumorista di equivalenti in moto
(Veli colorati, cartoni, stagnole, fili metallici, legno, tubi, pulegge)

DIREZIONE DEL MOVIMENTO FUTURISTA - Corso Venezia, 61 - MILANO

Umberto Boccioni, *Unique Forms of Continuity in Space*, 1913.

Notebook page with the addresses of Archipenko and Alexandra Exter.

The first and last page of the manifesto *The Futurist Reconstruction of the Universe*, signed by Balla and Depero, 11 March 1915.

"Marchesa Casati with mica eyes and a wooden heart, plastic ensemble, portrait by the Futurist Balla", 1915. From the periodical *Il Mondo*, 1919.

33

1914-1915. Words in freedom

The manifesto *Parole in libertà* (*Words in Freedom*) was launched by Marinetti in 1913. It opens with one of his splendid plates in which letters or numbers become dynamic images. Against D'Annunzio's poetry he proclaims freedom for typography and a "chain of pictorial sensations and analogies". One of the first to respond to Marinetti's appeal was Boccioni, who in November 1913, in the magazine *Lacerba*, published "Scarpetta da società + orina" ("Dress Slipper + Urine"), a page combining irony and provocation.
One of Balla's many experiments in this field was an advertising poster for a 1915 exhibition: the colours are luminous and the words all have personalities (note the word "cervello", "brain", written like the organ it represents). The letters of the alphabet fit together to create a picture.
An artist particularly active in this line was Francesco Cangiullo, a habitué of Balla's studio and not by chance one of the exhibitors at the Dadaist Café Voltaire in Zurich in 1917. And it was Depero, another pupil launched by Balla, who continued these experiments in the Twenties, successfully bringing together image, advertisement and typography.

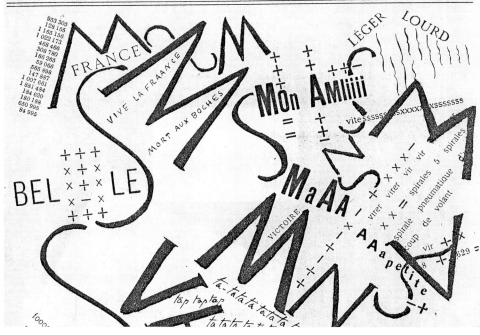

Manifesto *Words in Freedom* by F.T. Marinetti, 11 February 1915.

Umberto Boccioni, "words in freedom" plate. From *Lacerba*, November 1913.

Francesco Cangiullo, letter to Balla in the shape of a portrait of the artist, 6 February 1915.

Publicity for Fortunato Depero's Casa d'Arte
Futurista, 1925.

Poster by Balla for the exhibition at the Sala Angelelli, December 1915. Watercolour on paste-board.
Private collection.

Marinetti's book of "words in freedom", printed
on tin by Tullio d'Albisola, 1932.

1914-1917. From stage to screen

In the climate of "words in freedom" and happenings of 1914, Balla staged a "theatrical synthesis", *Macchina tipografica* (*Printing Press*), which had a gigantic word as a set and mannequins or robots as characters. But it was in the 1917 season that he achieved his theatrical ideal: *Feu d'artifice* with Stravinsky's music was put on at the Costanzi Theatre in Rome by Diaghilev's Ballets Russes (in February, seven of Balla's paintings had been included in an exhibition of the dancer Leonid Massine's collection).

This is how Margherita Sarfatti recalled the evening: "Neither painted backdrops nor people on stage — only forms. Constructed of wood and fabric, sharply angled shapes or reversed cones [...] projected asymmetrical shadows and light on the stage in correspondence with Stravinsky's enharmonic chords. The strange show lasted no more than five minutes and was composed exclusively of the two etheric vibrations, light waves and sound waves."

This was an abstract staging (shown in a photograph by Alfredo de Giorgi reproduced here for the first time), with a five-minute action based entirely on variations of light playing over the brilliantly coloured set. The synthesis of geometry-light-colour-movement lasted for a moment and dissolved with the applause.

Balla also signed the cinema manifesto and appeared in *Vita futurista*, a film directed by Ginna which foreshadows modern experimental work. Balla organized a scene in which he married a chair and a footstool was born, entitled "Marriage with the Object", and a scene with a dancer who melts into the backdrop in front of the artist. The cinema gave him a chance to finally achieve the union of light and movement, the two poles of his research from the outset.

Balla in the film *Vita futurista*, advertisement page published in *L'Italia Futurista*. Three frames from the "Dance of geometric splendour" and a frame from the episode "Balla marries a chair and a footstool is born."

Stage set and costume for *Macchina tipografica*, "noise-ist onomatopoeia", 1914.

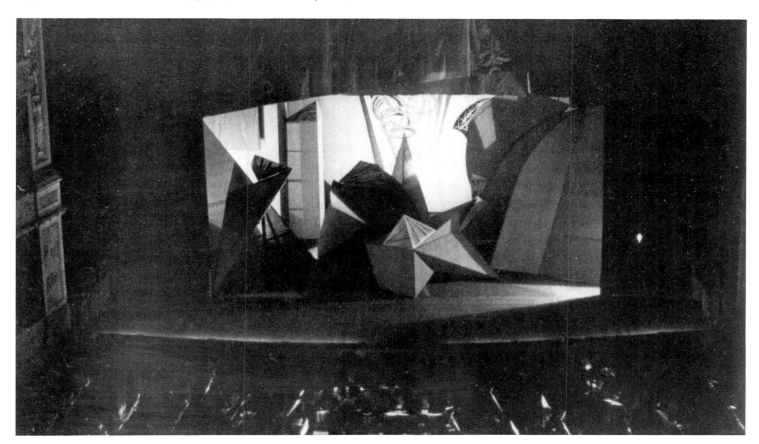

The first night of *Feu d'artifice* staged by Diaghilev's Ballets Russes at the Costanzi Theatre in Rome, April 1917 (photo by Alfredo de Giorgio).

1914-1925. Exhibitions in Europe and the United States

From the start Balla's work was shown not only in Europe, but also in America. In 1915 there was an exhibition in San Francisco, recorded in a photograph where his "Speeding Cars" can be glimpsed behind Boccioni's rhetorical sculpture. After the war he showed in Geneva, in the "Exposition internationale d'art moderne" (December 1920), and then in 1921 in Paris, in an exhibition for which he designed the poster. This was the period of Dadaism's triumph in Paris and the resulting controversy between Marinetti and the new prophets of the avant-garde. In 1925 he took part in the "Exhibition of Italian Art" in New York and in 1929 he was in Paris again, for the Futurist show organized by Gino Severini.

Most importantly, Balla kept in contact with a number of European artists. It was in his Rome studio that Michel Seuphor wrote the text of *L'éphémère est éternel*, for which settings were designed by Piet Mondrian. Balla wrote to him in Paris and Seuphor later recalled his painting, perhaps forgotten because it was too much ahead of its time.

Another fruitful connection was the friendship with Theo van Doesburg, to whom Balla wrote in the Twenties and who bought one of his "dynamic" paintings, subsequently re-sold to Peggy Guggenheim. As for his presence in England, it should be noted that London was the second destination of the exhibition of Futurist painters (March 1912, Sackville Gallery). In April 1914, with Marinetti present, the "Exhibition of the Works of the Italian Futurist Painters and Sculptors" opened. Balla showed ten canvases on the subject of dynamism — of automobiles, light and the sky. *Density of Atmosphere* is a masterpiece of 1913 (reproduced here on p. 42) which may have been sold in that show and has never reappeared.

A few months later, in July 1914, Ezra Pound published the Vorticist manifesto in the magazine *Blast*. Wyndham Lewis, Jacob Epstein and the others were to make good use of Futurism's concept of energy.

Poster with *Boccioni's Fist* for the Futurists' exhibition in Paris, 1929-30.

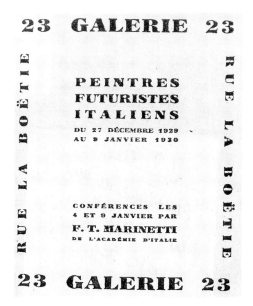

Catalogue of the Futurist exhibition in Paris, 1923.

Picasso in a Roman *osteria* in 1917.

Postcard from Balla to Theo Van Doesburg, c. 1925.

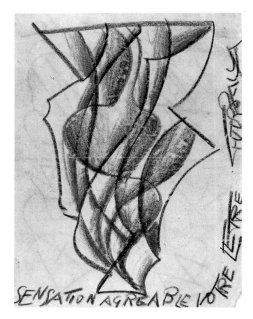

Works shown in the San Francisco exhibition in 1915: on the back wall, left, Balla's "Speeding Car" paintings.

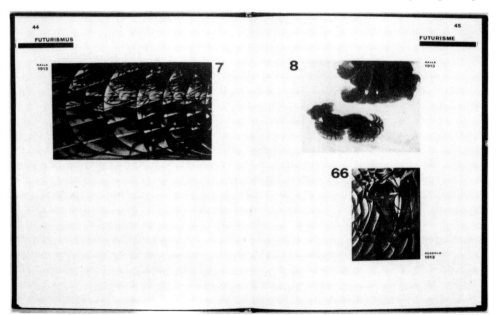

Two pages from the book by El Lissitsky and Hans Arp, *Die Kunstismen - Les ismes de l'art - The Isms of Art*, 1925.
Two paintings by Balla are reproduced: *Abstract Speed*, 1913, *and Dynamism of a Dog on a Leash*, 1912.

Postcard from Balla to Michel Seuphor (June 1926), when Seuphor was preparing the play *L'éphémère est éternel* with Mondrian's settings.

1914-1930. From celestial forces to "aeropittura"

The dynamic lines of vortices began to connect the reality of the earth with the movements of the cosmos. In 1914 Balla painted a remarkable series of canvases on the theme of "Mercury Passing in Front of the Sun Seen through a Telescope". An amateur astronomer since his youth, he now began to explore the mysteries of celestial dynamism, as in *Densities of Atmosphere* (*Spessori di atmosfera*).

The series of "Forms-Spirits Transformations" works present the relationship between earth and heaven mediated by spirituality (expressed by coloured triangles) a delicate mystery.

Already almost exhausted, Marinetti's Futurism resurfaced in September 1929 with the manifesto on "aeropittura", signed by Balla together with Benedetta, Depero, Dotti, Fillia, Marinetti, Prampolini, Somenzi and Tato. But its followers remained schematic and cold, while Balla continued to explore the poetry of colour and painting. *Celestial Metallic Aeroplane* (*Celeste metallico aeroplano*), celebrating the aviator Balbo, recalls his early studies of swifts, lines of speed and the interpenetration of colours.

Densities of Atmosphere, 1913. Oil on canvas. Present whereabouts unknown (disappeared in London, 1914).

Forms-Spirits Transformation, c. 1916. Oil on canvas. Private collection.

Mercury Passing in Front of the Sun, 1914. Oil on paste-board. Musée National d'Art Moderne, Centre Georges Pompidou, Paris.

The first "aeropittura" exhibition, Rome, January 1931.

One of the works exhibited: *Celestial Metallic Aeroplane (Balbo and the Trans-oceanic Aviators)*, c. 1930. Oil on wood. Museo dell'Aeronautica, Vigna di Valle (Rome).

1916-1918. Crisis of Futurism

The peak of Futurist enthusiasm was probably reached during the interventionist moment of 1915. When Boccioni left for the war, it became evident that things were changing. The only one to keep his memory alive seemed to be Balla, with his continual replicas of *Boccioni's Fist*. The death of his ex-pupil (commemorated with touching words and drawings by Severini, Marinetti and Carrà, as well) seemed to close the heroic period of Futurism.

Only Balla continued to experiment, but he changed his subject-matter and cycle. In October 1918, when he showed forty canvases painted during the war period, it was clear that he had gone back to his concern with the forces of nature. The gallery owner, Anton Giulio Bragaglia, in an article in his magazine *Cronache d'Attualità*, divided the paintings into three groups.

The first is represented by "landscape lines of force", modified by the state of mind when the mental vision superimposes itself on the physical eye. ("Looking at the same landscape, Balla has influenced it with different colours and distortions suggested by his mental vision.")

The second is that of "movimentismo" ("a form of exploration that the Bragaglia brothers have defined with their photographs of movement").

The third group is composed of "manifestations" ("architectural expressionism of the masses and volumes of voices").

Accentuatedly abstract and decorative, these canvases mark a moment of change in Balla's work. One reason for this was that he had remained the only major figure in the Futurist movement — Carrà was attracted by primitivism, and then in 1917 by de Chirico's metaphysics, Russolo had given up painting and Severini had gone back to spelling out the Cubist alphabet.

Balla continued to exhibit, but feeling less and less sure of his work. His important shows included the great Futurist exhibition at Palazzo Cova in Milan in 1919, a room (beside Boccioni) at the 1925 Rome Biennial, and a hall in the exhibition at the Amatori e Cultori in 1928 (93 paintings including *Pessimismo e ottimismo*, considered by Marinetti Balla's masterpiece, which document his whole life as a painter).

Boccioni at the front, in a 1915 photograph.

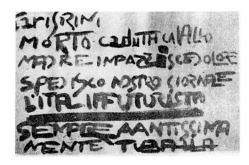

Postcard by Balla to Severini announcing the death of Boccioni.

Announcement of Boccioni's death with Balla's drawing *The Italian Fist of Boccioni*. From *L'Italia Futurista*, August 1916.

Poster for the exhibition at Bragaglia's gallery (1918) with a stylized *Boccioni's Fist*.

FORZE-PAESAGGIO

Two pages of Bragaglia's catalogue with the painting *Landscape Forces* and the *Manifesto of Colour*.

Primaverilis, c. 1918. Oil on canvas with original frame. Private collection.

1925. Art Déco

Giacomo Balla had always been concerned with decorative values — alongside his experiments with pure language he was always conscious of the presence of art in daily life. And in a certain sense the 1925 Paris exhibition seemed to confirm the correctness of his intuition. At the great "Exposition des arts décoratifs", which aimed to present the forces of "Modernism", he was a major exhibitor in the Italian pavilion alongside his pupils Depero and Prampolini. But in reality his work was a dialogue with the liveliest artists represented there, such as Sonia Delaunay and Pierre Legrain. This was also his last journey. He appears in a photograph on the Eiffel Tower, beside Depero.

Among the comments on the Paris exhibition there was a review by Margherita Sarfatti, who compared the Italian contribution to that of the Russians: "At the Paris Exhibition the spearhead of the artistic avant-garde was represented by the Soviets' pavilion and the Italian Futurist Section. On show there were designs for architectural ensembles, decorative objects and stage settings, by E. Prampolini and G. Balla, and panels by F. Depero."

Balla continued his experiments, of consistently high quality, in the field of the minor arts. This was work which he always saw as the necessary creation of an art for life after "art for art's sake". So his invented blooms aim to transform even natural flowers into joyously abstract constructions.

He created a great many designs for furniture (often inventive, like the "Children's Room" of 1914), and his ideas were applied by Depero. Balla's "overall" decorative projects included the cabaret *Bal Tik Tak*, opened in 1921 a few yards from the Palazzo delle Esposizioni; the spatial organization of the Casa d'Arte Bragaglia (inaugurated in its new site in Via degli Avignonesi in January 1922); and the decoration of Marinetti's house in 1925.

The poster of the "Art Déco" exhibition, Paris 1925.

On the Eiffel Tower in 1925: Depero, Balla and Iannelli.

A wall in the exhibition with four tapestries by Balla: *Butterflies and Futurist Flowers* (right and left), *Sea Sails Wind* (above), *Futurist Genius*.

Design for a children's room, 1914.
Private collection.

cuscini DEPERO
originalissimi - coloratissimi

Fortunato Depero's popular version of Balla's designs, from the book published by Depero in 1927.

The artist with his daughters Luce and Elica, beside his "Futurist Flowers", 1933.

The Thirties. The future of the past

It is not true that Balla denied his Futurist past. In 1933, for example, he contributed to the special issue of *Futurismo* in honour of Boccioni with a large drawing in his memory. From the paper we learn that amongst the supporters of the initiative were artists like Kandinsky, Mondrian, Brancusi, Cocteau, Picasso and Klee, together with dealers like Paul Guillaume and Léonce Rosenberg.

In reality, the young men launched by Marinetti who were practising religious art and "aeropittura" no longer interested Balla. In 1937 he declared to the magazine *Perseo*: "For several years I have been completely outside any Futurist events. I dedicated all my energy in complete faith and sincerity to the innovatory experiments, but at a certain point I found myself in the same camp as opportunistic, ambitious individuals whose interests were more commercial than artistic. I am convinced that pure art lies in absolute realism, without which one falls back into ornamental decorativism. So I returned to my earlier art: interpretation of bare, healthy reality, which seen through the spontaneous sensibility of the artist is always infinitely new."

The experimentalist had decided to change course. Balla gave up the painting which for twenty years had given him very little in exchange for all his youthful enthusiasm. His return to reality (but in a form that still reflects the meaning of the pictorial discoveries of those twenty years of work) was decided. This was a deliberate and honest step on the part of an inventor who saw the crowd of artists around him spoiling the germinal idea of Futurism.

Together with his wife and daughters, in 1926 he left his legendary studio in Via Paisiello. He went first to Villa Ambron and then in 1929 to Via Oslavia, where he was to live until his death. In 1935 he exhibited in Rome together with his daughters Luce and Elica, of whom he has left us touching portraits, just as they have of their father.

Boccioni portrayed by Balla on the front page of *Futurismo*, 11 June 1933.

46

We Four in the Mirror, 1946. Oil on canvas. Private collection.

The artist at his easel in 1947, in a photograph by Gjon Mili.

Balla with his guitar, in a painting by Luce Balla, 1943.

Portrait of the Artist's Daughter Luce, 1925. Crayon on paste-board. Private collection.

Portrait of the Artist's Daughter Elica, 1937. Oil on canvas. Private collection.

The postwar years. "Futurism forever"

In the last ten years of his life Balla enjoyed an increasing success, coming particularly from the United States, France and Switzerland. James Thrall Soby and Alfred Barr Jr. ensured a prominent role for him in the exhibition dedicated to Italian art in 1949 (New York, The Museum of Modern Art). He was among the major representatives in the Futurist exhibition at Zurich in 1950, while Christian Zervos gave him considerable space in his study on Italian art for the *Cahiers d'Art*, and subsequently organized a one-man show for him. Sandberg bought a "Car Speed" painting for the Stedelijk Museum, Amsterdam. In 1951 the Galleria Origine, founded by Piero Dorazio, Ettore Colla and other artists, gave him a solo showing with twenty works. Balla declared to a journalist: "Today I'm pleased but also rather astonished to be pulling out the old Futurist canvases I put aside twenty years ago. I thought those were things belonging only to my private story as an artist, but it seems they concern history as well..."
In 1954 came two shows in New York (Rose Fried Gallery, Sidney Janis Gallery). The first documentary volume of the *Archivi del futurismo* was published. Balla died on 1 March 1958 at the age of 87.
The year after his death, a large show devoted to Futurism opened in Rome, while in 1961, with the exhibition "Futurism" (New York, The Museum of Modern Art), Joshua Taylor confirmed the great relaunching of the movement. In the photograph by Sandberg, Balla appears in all his wisdom and irony.

A page written by Balla in 1920.

Two catalogues of American exhibitions, at the Rose Fried Gallery and the Sidney Janis Gallery, 1954.

SEMPRE FUTURISMO
ha! ha! che divertimento!
ha! ha! che superdivertimentissimo!
ih ih ih ih ih ih ih ih ih che ridere! e come
ridde questo FUTURISMO!! IH! OH! IH!
OH! IH! OH! gridano le somareschu!
a chi? e per chi? ha! ah! ah! ah!
che divertimentoooooooooo!
Sfrincibelluccoli, cimiciricabeccoli,
lallarillattemielici, pippififififichirin
=chigliniti, scappate, scappate, prima
che un soffio d'un futurista vi faccia
stramazzare a terra inton...ton. ton.
ton... tonitici _____

January 25 thru February 26, 1954

the
futurists
BALLA
SEVERINI
1912-1918
ROSE FRIED GALLERY
6 East 65 Street · New York

FUTURISM

Exhibition March 22 - May 1, 1954

Sidney Janis Gallery

15 East 57th Street New York 22

The artist photographed by C. Sandberg in front of *Abstract Speed*, Rome, 1952.

Catalogue of the works
in the exhibition

Note

All the data given in the technical descriptions of the works exhibited and/or reproduced here has been checked for this catalogue. Where it does not match with other studies (including those by the present author), the information given here should be taken as valid. Where the artist's name is not indicated in the captions, this means that the work is by Balla.
In the specifications of the works the following criteria have been used:

Title. This is the title inscribed on the work or the one under which it was first exhibited (any other titles are given in brackets). In the remaining cases the title has been attributed by induction, with reference to other works of the same period.

Dates. The date given is the one inscribed by the artist on the painting or the reverse, or in contemporary documents (there is no reason to doubt Balla's indications). In all other cases the date is preceded by a "c.", which means that the work oscillates slightly round the year given.

Measurement. The sizes are given height × width, in centimetres and (in brackets) inches.

Provenance. The indication "Casa Balla" is followed by the inventory number, if any. Only changes of ownership indicated in the exhibition catalogues or bibliography are listed.

Exhibitions. The indication of a catalogue- or page-number means that the work is reproduced, unless otherwise stated. The exhibition catalogues are included in the Bibliography. As far as possible, all the exhibitions have been listed. The Bibliography lists only the essential works (many publications are casual and often unimportant). Where a publication is indicated, this means that the work in question is reproduced there.

A number of exhibitions have been dedicated to Balla since his death. The most complete remains the one held in Turin in 1963, while the show in Rome (1971-72) was as ambitious as it was arguable. A few exhibitions have highlighted particular periods of his work (for instance, those coordinated by me in Rome in 1968). The most recent appearance of his work was in the Palazzo Grassi in Venice. There is no point in discussing the shows put on in private galleries since these have almost always been improvised, with selections of variable quality.

This catalogue on Balla was created to accompany to England a series of works chosen over more than a decade by a collector-dealer, Paolo Sprovieri. A first group was shown in Basel (1982), others in Zurich (1985), New York (1986), Edinburgh, London and Oxford (1987). One consideration guided the choice of the works: the realization that Balla's production represents a singular phenomenon over the span of our century. He is an experimentalist who tackled different themes and problems in the course of only a few months, moving with the naturalness of an acrobat from drawings to oils, from tempera to watercolour, from the project to the object. A commercial logic, supported by false historical justifications, has up to now imposed the pre-eminence of one technique over another, the feticism of oil on canvas, the presumption that a large-format work is more important than a smaller one.

The choice presented here, on the contrary, identifies the heart of the problem in the question of experimentation — analysis of light or synthesis of speed, vortex or interventionism, furnishing or decoration. In other words, it seeks the moment when the high quality of the result succeeds in conveying the maximum concentration of thought. In short, this exhibition is not intended to be just one more showing of Balla's work, but the indication of the most vital — and still relevant — points of his research.

M.F.

Balla's hand holding brushes. Detail of the painting *We Four in the Mirror* (*Noi quattro allo specchio*), 1946 (reproduced here on p. 49).

Abstractionist-Futurist

Balla was an inventor, magician, prophet, a leading figure in Italian culture in the 20th century — he compared himself with Leonardo or Titian. He abused the "passéist" artists who still set the standards for the time: "This past I so fiercely reject," he wrote in his notebook no. 4. But he could never bring himself to abandon a form of research which was also disciplined ("After working an artist should feel tired, excited, sometimes happy and nearly always dissatisfied"). This determined painter from Turin was always aware that his role was to be ahead of his time, contradicting the present and preparing the world of the future. In his initial period he tackled the problems of objective painting. Then he became one of the first to create an "abstract" work (1912); he built sculptures using perishable materials (1914); he achieved a synthesis of geometry-music-light-movement in a stage setting (designed in 1917 for the Ballets Russes); he tried to revolutionize people's clothing, furniture and behaviour. To all this must be added his experiments in the field of theatre, with "words in freedom", and his participation in the first Futurist film. Following the development of Balla's work takes us behind the scenes of Futurism, a movement which between 1909 and 1919 investigated practically every problem open to aesthetic research.

"Neither beauty nor ugliness have any limits now, since we are coming and going beyond the limits" — his lucid, futuristic axiom gives us an exact image of the great experimentalist. His working method was by definition experimental ("in the Cinquecento my name was Leonardo," Balla once wrote). He proceeded by "testing and re-testing", identifying problems that needed new solutions and then immediately searching for subsequent problems to be solved.

According to Balla (and the Futurists) the aim of art lies not in the discovery of Beauty but in the pure process of Research. Each of his works is an experiment, so there is no point in classifying his paintings according to the usual schemas (copy, replica, variations, prototype). Every scrap of paper may contain the flash of an idea. An "oil on canvas" often arises by pure chance. A piece of furniture may contain the idea for a painting just as a simple sketch may anticipate architecture. Even his manifestos about clothes or "plastic ensembles" are finished works in every sense. Because despite all the exhausting labour needed to create it, no object is ever completely achieved, nor does it aim to be. Every creation is only a project.

Balla is still a painter who is misunderstood or misvalued. One historian (De Marchis) who has studied Balla's multidimensional activity, states: "With a few rare exceptions, his major works were always exhibited shortly after he finished them. When they belong to a series, as is often the case, the paintings exhibited first can be considered the prototypes, although it is hard to identify them with any certainty within the vast set of studies, replicas and variants dedicated by Balla to practically every theme found in his work."

To this I would reply that the real point is not to see what Balla "wanted to be for his contemporaries", but rather what his contemporaries did *not* want him to be. Not in order to argue with the facts of history, but to see whether this history was not in reality rather more complex than the ordinary exhibitions make it appear.

It is a documented fact that the Futurists' works were presented at *soirées*, public events and casual meetings. There is no point in regretting that no catalogues have remained, since catalogues did not always exist. They were not Salon painters, but practical experimenters who enjoyed shocking public taste.

In Balla's case, moreover, it is impossible to develop a detailed, systematic description of his work. He was a painter who pretended to bury painting in order to invent a new dimension to work in every day. As soon as he caught the trick, he would immediately abandon the work in progress and begin another, which might then be exhausted for him one month or one work later. We cannot distinguish positivistically between "prototypes", "studies", "replicas" and "variants". This may be true of any other artist, but in the case of an experimentalist it is very obvious.

We need only remember that Balla's studio was open to everybody, that Futurism was not popular with the public, and that Balla's was not a "private" story since he succeeded in drawing dozens of artists into his orbit. When the Rome group took over the leadership of Futurism, Balla was their prophet. This was certainly not because of works shown in the Salons. And then, apart from anything else, there is the extraordinary quality of his work — quality of invention and execution.

Balla was the author of a series of cycles that follow each other like the waves of a tide, eagerly overlapping. Only today can we understand and study those "waves", after the analysis of his notebooks and all the work which until recently, by an incredible fate (Balla sold only one or two paintings from his Futurist period) had remained in his pyrotechnical house in Rome.

Notturno romano con lampione (Roman Night Scene with Street Lamp), c. 1902.

Lampione nel cantiere (Lamp on Construction Site), c. 1904. Pastel on paper. Private collection.

Notturno sulla Villa Borghese (Night over Villa Borghese), c. 1905. Pastels on paper. Private collection.

Il lavoro (Work), 1902. Oil on canvas. Winston-Malbin collection, New York.

A district in Rome by night, with the figure of a working-man, a street in perspective, a lamp casting light. This is the simple subject of a painting that tackles the modern theme of a night scene lit by what Marinetti a few years later called "divine electric light." Balla was nicknamed "Giacomo the night-bird" by his friends because of this interest, and in fact other works (reproduced here) also show how moonlight or a street lamp could become for him the centre of the picture.

Work (Il lavoro) — today in the United States — should in a certain sense be read together with his marvellous *The Workingman's Day* (reproduced here). The subject is not the workingman (in fact this painting dedicated to work ends up by portraying complete immobility), but the arc of the day — in other words, light. The two basic moments are full light (midday) and absence of light, followed by artificial light (night and the street lamp). In the preparatory studies the lamp appears decidedly in the foreground and is the pivot of the composition.

In an autobiographical sketch of 1920 Balla recalled his night work: "He was seen in Via Veneto standing motionless and studying tenaciously for over a year, every night — in fine weather, wind, rain, heat and cold — in order to understand all the gradations, the colourings that follow one another during the different seasons... From this study emerged a work with a night substance that was quite new."

Pastels on paper, 44 × 54 (17³/₈ × 21¹/₄).
Signed lower left: BALLA.
Provenance: private collection, Roma.
Exhibitions: New York, 1986, no. 1.

Elisa che cuce sul balcone (Elisa Sewing on the Balcony), c. 1904.

His wife is sewing a sheet on their balcony in Via Paisiello overlooking the trees of Villa Borghese: once again "simplicity" manifests itself. On this balcony a few years later Balla would contemplate the dynamic steps of his little girl — *Girl × Balcony* (*Bambina × balcone*) is the original title of the painting — or he would move to catch the sinous line of swifts in flight. His method is rooted in his need to achieve an elimination of all that is superfluous, an extraction-abstraction of spirituality from corporeality. In a letter from Paris dated 1899 he wrote: "Simplicity — a word much used but hardly ever applied — is the basis of beauty. This is always produced by the perfect truth of the elements and all great works have manifested themselves through very simple technical means."

In Paris he refined this simplicity of technical means by a careful study of Pointillism, which with its supreme analysis was the only technique able to synthesize movement and light.

Balla with his wife Elisa and their daughter Luce on the balcony in Via Paisiello around 1910.

Pastels on paper, 38 × 29.5 (15 × 11¹/₈).
Signed lower left: BALLA.
Provenance: private collection, Roma.

Aratro nella campagna (*Plough in the Campagna*), c. 1904.

Cantano i tronchi (*The Tree Trunks Are Singing*), 1906. Pastel on paper. Private collection.

Giacomo Balla playing the guitar. Photo taken around 1910.

To explore the simple force-forms of nature Balla went into the Roman Campagna several times. There he could study "en plein air" — in this case, a plough which the "objective" focus turns into an almost unnatural (metaphysical) object.

As in the great European Symbolist current, nature becomes the centre of a grand symphonic movement. A painting from this cycle (reproduced here) is called *The Tree-trunks Are Singing* (*Cantano i tronchi*). The state of mind is superimposed on the eternal flow of nature to rediscover a rhythm which is sometimes even sacred.

His portrait during those years of study is sketched in an autobiographical note written in 1920: "THE LATE BALLA — A short man, he wore an extremely thin cloak which he wrapped round his rosy face, very bright periwinkle-blue eyes and reddish-blond beard. He never spoke and was always alone. He would walk along the street stopping every ten steps to observe and think; on scraps of paper he traced mysterious, incomprehensible signs. [...] His friends were the people despised and rejected by everybody: madmen, beggars, the sick — rejects of society."

Pastels on paper, 29 × 43 (11¹/₂ × 17).
Signed lower right: BALLA.
Provenance: private collection, Roma.
Exhibitions: New York, 1986, no. 3.

Villa Borghese, c. 1904.

L'ombra sul prato (*The Shadow on the Lawn*), c. 1906. Pastel on paper. Private collection, Roma.

Interior of the studio in Via Paisiello around 1908 with a group of Divisionist paintings.

In his studio (reproduced here) the paintings which had nature as their subject multiplied, while he focused more and more patiently on the rhythm of his subjects, described in his titles as "spring shoots" or "ploughed earth". At this point Villa Borghese was his Mont Sainte-Victoire, the last image of nature in an increasingly demented urban scene.

"Simplicity is the basis of beauty" — this old motto of Balla's was to remain one of his basic commandments throughout his life. Even when he broke down movement and light, even when he came to abstract painting, even when he designed a new type of environment and its decoration.

To Balla, Villa Borghese was the landscape he could see from his window. Even the earliest "Iridescent Interpenetrations" began from the eucalyptus he had in front of his balcony. Only the artist who has started from nature's most secret nerves can reach the frontier of abstraction — this happened to Mondrian, too.

Pastels on paper, 28 × 35 (11 × 13³/4).
Provenance: private collection, Roma.
Exhibitions: New York, 1986, no. 2.

Gambe in movimento (*Legs in Movement*), 1912.
(Study for *Bambina che corre sul balcone*).

In the paintings Balla produced during the first decade of this century the fundamental importance of dynamism in his work can already be glimpsed. It is implicit in his choice of a Divisionist technique — the brushstrokes seem to pursue one another, the dabs of paint are drawn out lengthwise and pulsate like bacteria (semi-colons, lines, trajectories).

Over a few months in 1912 he carried out an analysis of movement in three paintings: May, Montepulciano: *Dynamism of a Dog on a Leash* (*Dinamismo di un cane al guinzaglio*); August, Rome: *Girl Running on a Balcony* (*Bambina che corre sul balcone*); November, Düsseldorf: *Rhythms of the Violinist* (*La mano del violinista*).

In a letter written in 1951 to Guido Le Noci he explained the reasons behind his research: "Note that *Dog on a Leash* was my first 'analytical' study of objects in movement, an 'indispensable' starting-point for discovering abstract lines of speed. Like the first lines of moving cars, initially objective and then synthetic, these are the basic foundations of my thought-forms."

Balla had gone to Montepulciano at the request of a young pupil in order to paint her roses which were just coming into bloom. He returned to Rome with the painting of her dog instead. But he had also acquired a new awareness and dropped the aim of art as an end in itself. He was now thinking in terms of pure research and prolonged experimentation. The painting of the *Girl Running*, for example, was preceded by about ten studies, which become increasingly complex until he reaches abstraction. Even the titles given to the works show that his procedure was scientific and mathematical as well as artistic. The can-

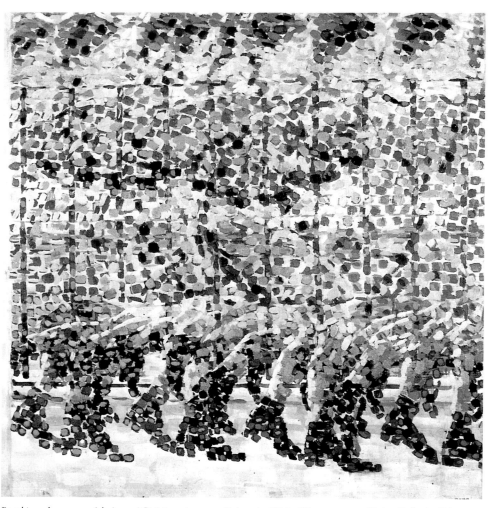

Bambina che corre sul balcone (*Girl Running on a Balcony*), 1912. Oil on canvas. Civica Galleria d'Arte Moderna, Milano.

vas painted in his Rome terrace was, in fact, called *Girl × Balcony* (*Bambina × balcone*) at its first showings; in this visions and sensations are multiplied (immediately afterwards they will be added together or divided up).

Charcoal on paper, 32 × 44 (12⅝ × 17⅜).
Signed and titled on the back.
Provenance: Casa Balla, no. 341.
Exhibitions: Torino, 1963, no. 53; Roma, 1968; Roma, 1971, no. 18; Wien, 1985, no. 12; Zürich, 1985, no. 1; New York, 1986, no. 4.
Bibliography: *Archivi del Futurismo*, 1962, no. 36b; Barricelli, 1967, no. 30; Lista, 1982, no. 289.

Studio di ruote in movimento (*Study of Moving Wheels*), c. 1912.

Salutando (*Waving*), c. 1908. Oil on canvas. Winston-Malbin collection, New York.

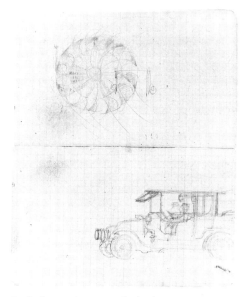

Study for moving car and wheel, c. 1912. Two sheets from Notebook no. 5.

Dinamismo di cane al guinzaglio (*Dynamism of a Dog on a Leash*), 1912. Oil on canvas. Knox Art Gallery, Buffalo (USA).

His exploration starts from a minute analysis (of a car wheel in this case) which quickly turns into a synthesis (abstract speed). All the preparation for his research is recorded in a few precious notebooks where the artist jotted down his progress as though he were keeping a diary (the notebooks have been published in facsimile: *I taccuini di Balla nos. 4, 3, 5*, edited by M. Fagiolo, Martano, Torino, 1982-86). It is fascinating to follow Balla through the stages of his work. First he makes a careful study of single elements (the car wheel, the driver's silhouette), then he works out the colour (on one page the word "brown" is written because he discovered that movement cancels speed and so in the most intense of these paintings ended up by using monochrome). Finally there comes a synthesis (the shape of the car is combined with noise, light and the environment).

His need to discover this new subject of dynamic movement was already implicit in his work during the decade preceding Futurism. A painting like *Waving* (*Salutando*) takes optical experimentation to an extreme bordering on hallucination. The judgement of a journalist at the Esposizione di Belle Arti in 1910 was symptomatic: "I won't discuss that *Waving*, which is more of a photograph than a painting." The unexpected cutting focuses attention on the flow of the steps — an analytical image of movement. The staircase with the three women turned towards the top has the value of a dream allusion (an attitude that should be borne in mind in any study of this experimentalist).

Blue crayon on paste-board, 25 × 38.5 (9⁷/₈ × 15¹/₈).
Signed lower right: BALLA.
Provenance: Casa Balla.
Exhibitions: Torino, 1963, no. 78, fig. 23b.
Bibliography: Lista, 1982, no. 225.

Compenetrazione iridescente (*Iridescent Interpenetration*), study I, c. 1913.
Compenetrazione iridescente (*Iridescent Interpenetration*) study II, c. 1913.

Two studies for iridescent interpenetrations based on a circular motif. From the *Düsseldorf Notebook*, 1912-13.

In these two cases the analysis of light is organized in a circular pattern. The sense of atmospheric dust is the result of a complex consideration of the overlapping studies of this period: the modular swifts' wings, the dynamism of the wheels of a moving car. As always with Balla, the passage from analysis to synthesis is immediate.

The search for pure colour was an important concern of European art in these prewar years. In Paris, Delaunay had experimented with breaking down colour-light. Severini was soon to come up with a similar decomposition: this was inevitable, considering that — like Balla — he had started from the Divisionist technique. A letter from Picasso to Soffici (20 April 1915) is also symptomatic: "Anyway, the time has come to really look at colour; it mustn't be only a garment, we need to understand the world of colour." Speaking here is the man who theorized colour as a

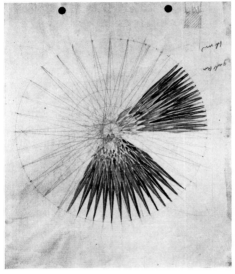

state of mind (the Blue and Pink periods) and the monochrome painter (the brown and grey of the first Cubist period).

Watercolour and pencil on paper, 16.5 × 24 (6½ × 9½).
Watercolour on paper, 12.5 × 19 (4⅞ × 7½).

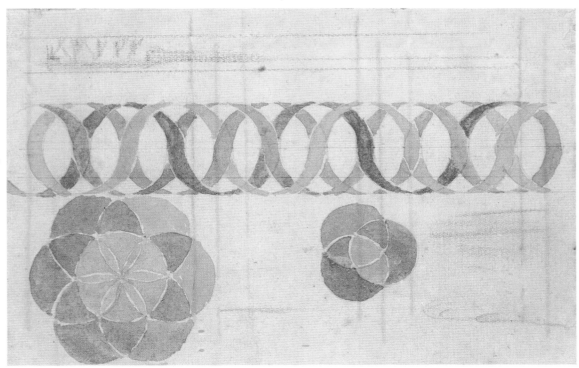

Compenetrazione iridescente (*Iridescent Interpenetration*), study, c. 1913.

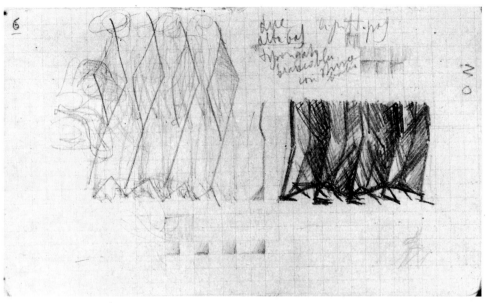

Study for legs in movement and break-down of light, 1912. Sheet from Notebook no. 5.

Compenetrazione iridescente (*Iridescent Interpenetration*). Card sent to Sibilla Aleramo, 8 April 1913.

Another analytical phase, begun in Düsseldorf in 1912, was developed further in 1913 with Balla's poster for the Rome exhibition of the "Secession" and a series of paintings (one was shown in the foyer of the Costanzi Theatre in February). It continued in 1914 as a theme of research to be combined with other explorations (cf. M. Fagiolo, *Le compenetrazioni iridescenti*, Roma, 1968).

A drawing (reproduced here) illustrates in a single notebook page how his search for the line of movement could be combined with his search for the line of light. The break-down into successive triangles in fact starts from the rhythm of moving legs and ends up representing the purity of the rainbow.

Balla does not merely demonstrate the fact that light has a triangular form, as in his *Street Light* (*Lampada ad arco*). By a return to the optics of the spectrum (red interpenetrates with blue, green, yellow, orange and violet), light is purified and reconstructed on a strict basis in order to rediscover the value of the rainbow as a symbol of light. The interpenetration effect is an application of the scientific principle of the speed of light.

We know his research started towards the end of 1912 in Düsseldorf, where he was working in the Löwenstein house on the banks of the Rhine. The first "little prism" which he sent to his family in a letter of December 1912 was accompanied by an explanation of his research. The study of the anatomy of light starts from his usual analysis of nature ("observation from life"), represented in this particular case by the rainbow. But beyond this there is also his passion for experimentation (he talks about "testing and re-testing"), his aim of achieving simplicity, and a playful intention (he mentions "delight"). In his letters to his family we can feel that abstraction will be the inevitable outcome. He talks about effects "that it would be better to consider unpaintable": mountains reflected in water on the Italian border, the pointed architecture of Düsseldorf, poplars against the sky, Gothic arches, the curves of an iron bridge reflected in the Rhine. Basically he is interested in the facts of the landscape modified by light ("The quality of the light makes everything more mysterious and veiled, matter becomes less real").

His research also embraces symbolic values. The triangle and circle are geometrical emblems representing perfection and the cosmos — mystical signs of the infinite. The triangle is the perfect hermetic form of light, but is has also been proved that the "v" shape corresponds scientifically to the sign of the speed of light. And the mirror effect of the triangles is also scientific, as a principle connected to the spectrum.

Watercolour on paper, 24 × 18 (9¹/₂ × 7¹/₂).
Provenance: Casa Balla; Maurizio Fagiolo, Roma.
Exhibitions: Roma, 1968; Venezia, 1968; Düsseldorf, 1974; Modena, 1979, p. 39; Zürich, 1985, no. 12; New York, 1986, no. 15.
Bibliography: Fagiolo, 1967, p. 43a; Fagiolo, 1968 (1970, part II) p. 41, no. 54; Dortch Dorazio, 1970, no. 75a; Fagiolo, 1982, p. 63; Block, 1975, cover.

Compenetrazione iridescente N. 4 - studio della luce (*Iridescent Interpenetration No. 4 - Study of Light*), c. 1913.

Compenetrazione iridescente (*Iridescent Interpenetration*), c. 1912. Watercolour on paper. Private collection.

His earliest study of light was in the painting *Street Light* (*Lampada ad arco*; reproduced here on p. 19). Balla chose it for the first Futurist exhibition in Paris although the canvas was not in fact shown. This work, still very striking today, marks the crowning achievement of the careful study of light he made in his Divisionist period. This is no longer a metaphor of light but the attempt to render pictorially the real effect of a Voltaic arc lamp, at that time a novelty in Rome. There is the obsessive repetition of a single motif in a serial geometry with no variations (this will also be the case with the violinist's hand, the dog's tail and the little girl's legs). In other words, light is closely linked with movement in a synthesis recalling the scientific principle of the "speed of light". This is derived from relativity, but corresponds equally to the technique of the cinema, also based on a synthesis of light and movement. Above the street lamp shines the crescent moon (already present in all the preparatory drawings): natural and artificial light are brought together and the artificial triumphs over the natural, the human over the metaphysical. "Let's kill moonlight", as the Futurist manifesto said.

On this subject there is a letter from Balla replying to Alfred Barr Jr. when the latter was buying the painting for the Museum of Modern Art in New York in 1954: "I painted the *Street Light* canvas during my Divisionist period (1900-1910). In fact the glow of the light is obtained by placing pure colours side by side. This painting, besides being original as a work of art, is also scientific because I tried to represent light by separating it into its component colours. It is of great historical interest both for its technique and its subject. Nobody at that time (1909) thought that a banal electric light could be the subject of a painter's inspiration. But for me there was a reason: I was interested in the representation of light, and above all I wanted to show that romantic 'moonlight' had been defeated by the light of the modern electric lamp. In other words, it was the end of romanticism in art: the phrase 'Let's kill moonlight' came from my painting. Rendering light has always been my particular interest. The painting of the *Street Light* was shown in Rome at one of the first Futurist exhibitions, in the foyer of the Costanzi Theatre. Those early improvised shows, organized with limited means, often had no catalogue

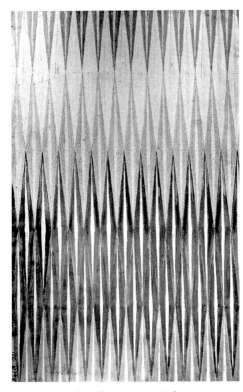

Compenetrazione iridescente n. 1 (*Iridescent Interpenetration no. 1*), 1912. Oil on canvas. Winston-Malbin collection, New York.

— and anyway I was always very busy studying artistic problems and didn't bother to collect catalogues. As regards the installation of electric street lighting in Rome, I asked the Technical Office of the Municipality for information and was told that those lamps (Brunt models) were already lighting the main streets of the city in 1904, before they had come into use in America or England. The one I painted was in Piazza Termini."

Oil on paper, 55 × 76 (21⁵/₆ × 30).
Signed upper left: BALLA. On the back: COMPENETRAZIONE IRIDESCENTE N. 4 - STUDIO DELLA LUCE.
Provenance: Casa Balla; Galleria Blu, Milano; Galleria Notizie, Torino.
Exhibitions: New York (Rose Fried), 1954, no. 2; Torino, 1963, no. 60; Torino, 1967; Frankfurt, 1963, no. 4; Paris, 1973, no. 3; Basel, 1982, p. 23; Zürich, 1985, no. 10; New York, 1986, no. 13; Vancouver, 1986, no. 4.
Bibliography: *Archivi del Futurismo*, 1962, no. 53; Ballo, 1964, p. 71; Calvesi, 1967, p. 108; Fagiolo, 1968 (1970, part II), p. 43, no. 4; Martin, 1968, p. 176; Lista, 1984, no. 1088.

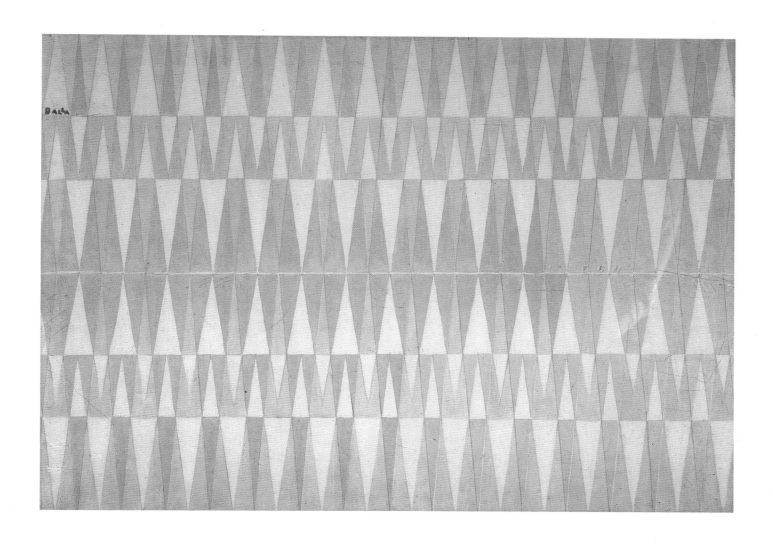

Compenetrazione (Interpenetration), c. 1913.

 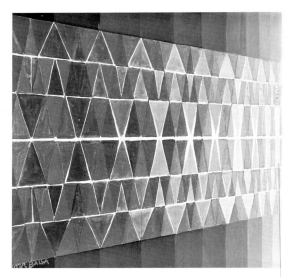

Study for *Compenetrazione iridescente* (*Iridescent Interpenetration*) with self-portrait, c. 1913. Watercolour on paper. Civica Galleria d'Arte Moderna, Torino.

Compenetrazione iridescente no. 9 (*Iridescent interpenetration no. 9*), c. 1913. Tempera on paper. Civica Galleria d'Arte Moderna, Torino.

Balla's research became more complex: to the subject of light was added that of the ray. He made a number of experiments in which the triangles reflect one another, and run down into slanting points that suggest the idea of movement. His research was also a "variation on a theme", in the exact musical meaning of the expression. Remembering the experimentation started in Düsseldorf, one can almost see the forty-year-old artist starting again from scratch, working on his exquisite coloured notebooks on a table in the music-room of the Löwenstein house, while beside him the owner practised his "violinist's hands".

In connection with this painting (which resurfaced in 1977), it is interesting to note that Balla told everybody about his research; so it was not a private, irrelevant study as a few later detractors have claimed. The discovery of the motif was communicated in a brightly coloured message to his family. From Düsseldorf he also sent his pupil Gino Galli a model of "interpenetration" to be developed in successive studies. And to Sibilla Aleramo, the companion of his friend Giovanni Cena, he sent the same motif on a card (reproduced here).

The painting discussed here was a gift to his pupil Francesco Cangiullo, who was particularly close to him during the war years. The colours shade from pale violet to blue in a layout that has a symbolic meaning: the format is in fact based on a double square, like the triangle an emblematical shape typical of this esoteric period of Balla's work.

Mixed media on paper (mounted on linen by the artist), 25 × 50 (9$7/8$ × 19$3/4$).
Dedicated right: A Cangiullo poeta FUTURISTA e amico mio BALLA. On the back of the canvas: COMPENETRAZIONE BALLA FUTURISTA. On the frame: Nathan Via Torino 122. White strip only.
Provenance: Giuseppe Milandri, Roma; Galleria dell'Obelisco, Roma-New York; Kouros Gallery, New York.
Exhibitions: Wien, 1985, no. 10; Zürich, 1985, no. 11; New York, 1986, no. 14; Venezia, 1986, p. 78.
Bibliography: Fagiolo, 1982, p. 65; Lista, 1984, no. 1084.

Penetrazioni dinamiche d'automobile (Dynamic Penetrations of a Car), c. 1913.

BALLA. – Penetrazioni dinamiche d'automobile
(1913)
Pénétrations dynamiques d'auto

A page from Boccioni's book *Pittura scultura futuriste*, 1914.

Penetrazioni dinamiche d'automobile (Dynamic Penetrations of a Car), c. 1913. Charcoal on paper. Private collection.

Only a passionate automobile fan or a FIAT public relations man could imagine that between 1913 and 1914 Balla was a painter of cars. In reality he used this modern pretext (in the same way as he used a little girl's legs, the wings of swifts, the forms of light or those of the wind, with vortices) simply to experiment with the subject of dynamism. It is difficult and methodologically incorrect to distinguish exactly between preparatory studies, pro-jects and finished works, because what counts for an experimentalist is the whole series of his experiments. In the case of the car subject, besides all the many studies in his notebooks, the works of his "testing and re-testing" (as Balla once defined his method) are about forty.

A number of paintings from the series were exhibited immediately in the Futurist ex-hibition organized by the magazine *Lacer-ba* in Florence in 1913; in the "Esposizio-ne di pittura futurista" at Sprovieri's Rome gallery; in the Futurist exhibition at the Doré Gallery in London, and finally in the "Panama Pacific International Exhibition" of 1915 in San Francisco. A few of the paintings are published in Boccioni's Fu-turist bible, *Pittura scultura futuriste*, which came out in February 1914, and in Soffici's important *Cubismo e futurismo* (1915).

The work analyzed here, as precise as an anatomical plate or a physics table, presents movement and its break-down. This mo-ment of Balla's exploration seemed to culminate in the painting reproduced by Boccioni (the page of the book is illustrated here). If Boccioni's publication, besides summing up Futurism, was also a point of departure for international research, this was only because it included Balla's paint-ings.

Charcoal on paper, 28 × 32.5 (11 × 12³/₄).
Signed lower left: FUTUR BALLA (stamped with the "Pugno di Boccioni").
Provenance: Casa Balla, no. 17.
Exhibitions: Vancouver, 1986, no. 2.

Velocità d'automobile (Car Speed), 1913.

Studies for a car standing still and then moving, 1912-13. Four pages from Notebook no. 5.

In a period concerned with issues very different from those in the car paintings (although the automobile was for Balla a temporary pretext for painting and not the point of his work — an object and not a subject), the report of a journalist is illuminating: "The artist explained his work by recalling that in 1913 he had wanted to render the movement of a car seen from the side. The old-fashioned type of car emerges from intersecting straight lines radiating from it in front, representing the expansion and noise of the motor. The curved lines and concentric circles which start from the car and run below and behind it are meant to give the impression of its speed and the blast of air, the sensations we have when a fast car goes by. A lady in a large hat and the driver are glimpsed as the main elements of dihedrons, polyhedrons and the curvilinear surrounding forms. The painting is practically monochrome and has great decorative intensity."

In Balla's paintings of speed the cars always move from right to left, and the densities of the atmosphere in another series increase in the same direction (in circular or diagonal forms). Since it is a scientific observation that the spectator reads the picture from left to right (at least in the West), this makes the impact between the subject represented and the spectator's eye more dynamic (here it is a speeding car, in another case it will be "Boccioni's Fist".)

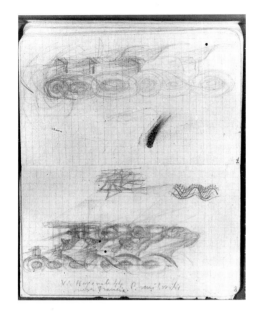

In the same way, when travelling on a train we are struck by the relative movement of the landscape but even more by the movement of another train coming from the opposite direction.

Oil on paper, 48 × 66.5 (19 × 26¼).
Signed lower left: FUTUR BALLA 1913.
Provenance: Casa Balla; Sidney Janis Gallery, New York.
Exhibitions: New York, 1954, no. 3; Basel, 1982, p. 21; Wien, 1985, no. 15; Zürich, 1985, no. 15; New York 1986, no. 18; Venezia, 1986, p. 80 .
Bibliography: Lista, 1984, no. 1079.

Plasticità di luci (Plasticity of Lights), c. 1913.

BALLA. – Plasticità di luci × velocità
(1913)
Plasticité de lumières × vitesse

A page from Boccioni's book *Pittura scultura futuriste,* 1914, with a version of *Plasticità di luci × velocità (Plasticity of Lights × Speed),* 1913.

Velocità d'automobile + luce (Car Speed + Light), c. 1913. Enamel on gold paper. Private collection.

In this work the decomposition of a car is combined with an interpenetration of light. The same title, *Plasticity of Lights × Speed (Plasticità di luci × velocità)* recurs in other paintings (the one published in Boccioni's book, for example) and we also find it in a notebook page with the variant "Plastic equivalents of luminosity in fast movement". Balla's studies on the break-down of light ("Iridescent Interpenetrations") began to bear fruit: like an alchemist, after isolating his forces he married them together in a search for gold.

The gold paper support was not a casual choice, since Balla used it on other occasions (as in the work reproduced here). The effect is most unpainterly.

This search for movement combined with light was intensified in another work of the series (today in The Museum of Modern Art, New York; repoduced here on p. 21) in which the car is refracted in a shop-window. It is the only brightly coloured version simply because the kaleidoscopic effect connects with the chromatic variety of the objects on display.

Oil and enamel on gold paste-board, 16 × 23 (6³/₄ × 9).
Signed lower left: BALLA. On the back: PLASTICITÀ DI LUCI BALLA (stamped with the "Pugno di Boccioni").
Provenance: Casa Balla, no. 395; private collection Milano; Kouros Gallery, New York.
Exhibitions: Torino, 1963, no. 82; Venezia, 1986a, no. 2; Vancouver, 1986, no. 3.
Bibliography: Archivi del Futurismo, 1962, no. 52; Lista, 1982, no. 328.

Velocità astratta (Abstract Speed), c. 1913.

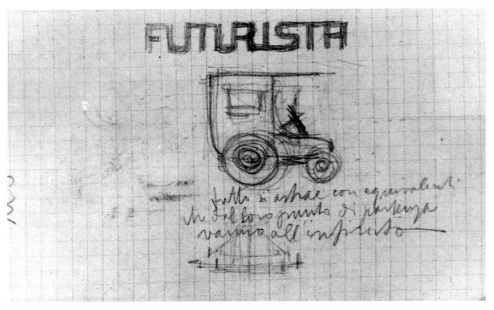

Sheet from Notebook no. 5. Beside the work "FUTURISTA" and a car drawn from life is written: "Everything abstracts itself with equivalents that go from their starting point to infinity."

Velocità astratta (Abstract Speed), c. 1913. Charcoal on paper. Private collection.

Balla's search for a synthesis was intensified at this point. The moving wheels become sequences of oval modules; the car's lines of penetration in the atmosphere are simplified in a criss-cross of straight and oblique lines resulting in triangles with different inclinations.

The idea of abstraction was already present in the artist's mind. In fact in a notebook page (reproduced here) we find the outline of a car not yet in movement, joined to the word "FUTURISMO" and a sort of commandment: "Everything becomes abstract, the equivalents go from a starting point to infinity."

Boccioni's exploration of "states of mind"

and "complementarism" was complicated by an "equivalent" of forms (a sort of psychological force-line) which he defined as "abstract".

In 1913 a journalist wrote: "Balla is working on a painting representing Via Nazionale in the exuberance and excitement of its traffic tumult. When he was working on *Bankruptcy* he spent hours standing in front of a closed door in Via Veneto. In the same way now, to study cars (the two or three that probably passed through the Roman street at that time) he feels the need to study 'en plein air'."

To be convincing, every abstraction must start from the force-forms of real life, says Balla. And Mondrian was also to say the same thing.

Charcoal on paper, 25 × 18 (9⁷/₈ × 7).
Signed lower right: FUTUR BALLA.
Provenance: Casa Balla; Maurizio Fagiolo, Roma.
Exhibitions: Wien, 1985, no. 13; Zürich, 1985, no. 18; New York, 1986, no. 21.

Velocità di motocicletta (*Motorcycle Speed*), c. 1913.

Velocità d'automobile astratta (*Abstract Car Speed*), c. 1913. Oil on paste-board covered with netting. Private collection.

Velocità astratta (*Abstract Speed*), c. 1913. Charcoal on paper. Private collection.

One of the subjects, or rather pretexts, initially chosen by Balla for his exploration of dynamism was the horse, as we see from his notebook pages, but he immediately discarded this symbolical form emphasized by Boccioni. The automobile became his central image, but he also used the motorcycle, as in this case. There is no mythology in Balla's exploration, no concession to the idea of the centaur, for instance. Balla's only myth remained that of dynamism and its abstraction.

In a perfect work like this one, apart from everything else, one sees how the forms chosen for the decomposition of the visible object (and the composition of the work) are very close to those used for light, the atmosphere, vortices and abstract speed.

Balla seemed to move almost alone along this path of "abstraction", the direction most open to the future. His ex-pupil Se-verini had always needed a connection to the image, but at the end of 1913 he seemed to shift his focus. In a letter to Sprovie-ri which links him to Balla, he wrote: "My latest painting is at Balla's. If you think it necessary, have it photographed. It's the work I find most satisfactory because it begins to connect my vision of form and colour. This is the basis of a new period of absolute abstraction for me."

Charcoal on paper, 50 × 70 (19³/₄ × 27⁵/₈).
Signed lower left: FUTUR BALLA.
Provenance: Casa Balla, no. 1265; Galleria L'Isola, Roma.
Exhibitions: New York, 1984, p. 24; Wien, 1985, no. 14; Zürich, 1985, no. 16; New York, 1986, no. 19.
Bibliography: Lista, 1984, n. 1077.

Linea di velocità astratta (*Abstract Line of Speed*), c. 1913.

Linea di velocità + paesaggio (*Speed Line + Landscape*), c. 1913. Oil on paper. Private collection.

Ritmo + velocità (*Rhythm + Speed*), 1913. Pastels on paper. Galleria Nazionale d'Arte Moderna, Roma (Balla Bequest).

This small study is interesting as one of the first formulations of the "abstract" line of speed. The supporting material should also be noted: a net laid over the wooden base which is not casual, since it reappears at least twice (in versions of his name and qualification "Futurist").

In another painting of 1913, the subject *Speed + Car + Lights* (*Velocità + auto + luci*) is represented with the same system.

For an observer of nature like Balla, a material can also prove useful for suggesting aspects that painting may not be able to render. The wide-meshed net becomes an effective filter for duplicating the idea of movement. These are devices commonly used later in Optical Art.

Collage is exploited by Balla in a similar way. It appears very early in his work, used first in an analytical and then in a decorative way. The insertion of coloured paper aims to extend the pictorial statement and simultaneously represents the insertion of an anti-pictorial element. The collage paper is therefore connected to the actual process of invention and its effect. It is never used in an "aesthetic" fashion as is the case in Cubism (and in Boccioni's work).

Oil on wood covered with netting, 12.5 × 29 (5 × 11³/₈).
Signed left: BALLA. On the back: LINEA DI VELOCITÀ ASTRATTA BALLA.
Provenance: Casa Balla; Galleria dell'Obelisco, Roma-New York; Kouros Gallery, New York.
Exhibitions: Roma, 1968; Torino, 1974, no. 14; Wien 1985, no. 20; Zürich, 1985, no. 19; New York, 1986, no. 23; Vancouver, 1986, no. 5.
Bibliography: *Archivi del Futurismo*, 1962, no. 140; Lista, 1982, no. 394.

Velocità + Paesaggio (Speed + Landscape), 1913.

Velocità astratta + rumore (Abstract Speed + Noise), 1913. Peggy Guggenheim collection, Venezia.

Velocità astratta, l'auto è passata (Abstract Speed, the Car Has Passed), 1913. Tate Gallery, London.

This work is one of the most important of Balla's studies on the dynamism of cars. As I pointed out some years ago, the painting was conceived together with two others. The first is *Abstract Speed, the Car Has Passed (Velocità astratta, l'auto è passata)*, today in the Tate Gallery, London. The second is in the Peggy Guggenheim collection, Venice, and is titled: *Abstract Speed + Noise (Velocità astratta + rumore)*; this painting was bought by Van Doesburg, like Severini's coeval *Danseuse = Mer*.

The car is combined with the rhythm of a landscape in a sort of "triptych of speed". This idea of continuity is obviously related to symbolist ideas, and passes through Divisionism (there are similar solutions by Boccioni and Balla), before reaching early Futurism (Boccioni's *States of Mind*).

Thus speed becomes form, almost the character of a play in three acts.

Oil on paste-board, 49 × 71 (19$^{1}/_4$ × 28). Original painted frame, 54 × 75.5 (21$^{1}/_4$ × 29$^{3}/_4$).
Below left: BALLA. On the back: BALLA VIA PAISIELLO 39 ROMA VELOCITÀ + PAESAGGIO BALLA 1913.
Provenance: Casa Balla (no. 40).
Exhibitions: Roma, 1951, no. 13.
Bibliography: *Il Futurismo*, 9 April 1933; *Archivi del Futurismo*, 1962, no. 62; Fagiolo, 1970, p. 27; Dortch Dorazio, 1970, no. 2; Lista, 1982, no. 312.

Linea di velocità (Line of Speed), c. 1913.

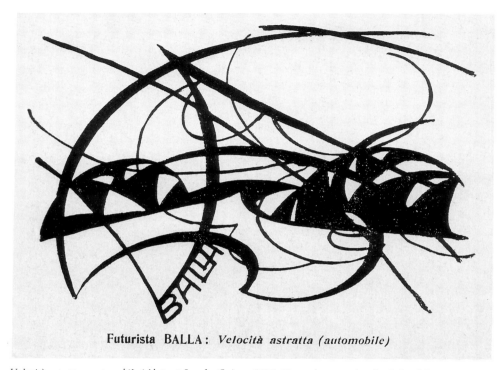

Futurista BALLA: *Velocità astratta (automobile)*

Velocità astratta - automobile (Abstract Speed - Car), c. 1913. From the magazine *La Balza*, Messina, 1915.

The "abstract line of speed" in a card sent to Marinetti.

Balla always aimed towards a synthesis, but he wanted to find it scientifically, following exhaustive analysis. After a great many separate studies (on relative motion, light, dynamism, flight, penetrations) he at last found his solution. This was the "line of speed", an all-embracing form recognizable only to a surreal mentality like his.

Works like the one exhibited here, or the intense painting today in the Toronto Museum, date from 1913. The "line of speed" is as precise and scientific as a demonstration in an engineering manual, but also as poetical as the sinuousness of Art Nouveau. It became a sort of definitive trademark in his works up to 1918. It is the most important form of his whole range and, as Balla put it, "the fundamental basis of my thought-forms". Besides expressing the excitement aroused by the modern mystery of speed, it is also an attempt to convey the structure of movement, the engineering design of dynamism.

In his notebook pages we can follow the line from its incubation to its clear definition. Immediately afterwards, in his paintings up to 1918, we see how he marries it to other motifs: a landscape, a sky, a vortex. As always, Balla alternates dynamism and immobility, subjectivity and objectivity, thinking and existing. The glorious trademark is thus tested against the artist's familiar world — the space of the earth and the mysteries of the atmosphere.

Charcoal on paper, 63 × 69.5 (24⁷/₈ × 27³/₈).
Signed lower left: FUTUR BALLA (stamped with the "Pugno di Boccioni").
Provenance: Casa Balla, Roma; private collection, Milano.

Ritmo + rumore + velocità d'automobile (*Rhythm + Noise + Car Speed*), 1913. Enamels on paper. Private collection.

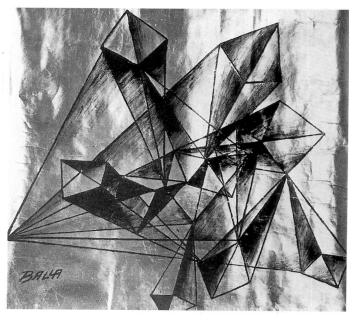

Forme rumore (*Noise Forms*), c. 1914. Enamel on gold paper. Private collection.

Abandoning the pretexts for his paintings — swifts, cars — Balla was left with his research text: the "line of speed". His new problem was how to combine it with other sensations. In this case Balla even tries to give form to an element coming from another sensory sphere, that of sound. So his perfect "line of speed" is married to zig-zag lines representing the idea of noise (Luigi Russolo, the inventor of "Noise Art", was a friend of Balla's).

The formulation of his "noise form" appears in a notebook and is expressed in abstract terms in a work on gold paper (reproduced here). The commercial gold-leaf can also serve to suggest light and noise. A marvellous painting of the same period is *Rhythm + Noise + Car-speed* (*Ritmo + rumore + velocità d'automobile*), reproduced here. This is another mathematical exercise in interpenetration. In this case the "noise forms" are represented by the ancient sign of the swastika (not yet notorious), which is in fact a symbol of light.

Oil on canvas, 30 × 47.5 (24³/₄ × 18³/₄).
Signed lower left: FUTUR BALLA.
Provenance: Casa Balla, no. 19; private collection, Milano.
Exhibitions: Roma, 1986, no. 1; New York, 1986, n. 22.

Paesaggio (Landscape), 1913.

Linee di forza di paesaggio + ametista (Landscape Force-lines + Amethyst), c. 1917. Oil on paper. Galleria Nazionale d'Arte Moderna, Roma (Balla Bequest).

Linee forza di paesaggio + sera (Landscape Force-lines + Evening), c. 1917. Oil on canvas. Private collection.

Balla's new problem can be stated in these terms: how to marry his synthetic "line of speed" to another sensation in order to continue his chain of analyses? Now he rediscovered the subject that had been his great source of inspiration earlier: the landscape. Already in 1913, as the work we are examining shows, the terms of his calculation were set out. The combination was to become systematic after his stage design for *Feu d'artifice* by the Ballets Russes — a sort of global landscape modified by light. Between 1917 and 1918 he painted an extraordinary series of canvases, fifteen of which were shown in October 1918 in his exhibition at the Casa d'Arte Bragaglia. The form is always the same — the "line of speed" which was the outcome of his previous search for "equivalents" — but each time it is combined with a different heterogeneous element. The titles of the paintings in the exhibition illustrate the variety of the associations: "dust", "horse chestnuts", "water-melon", "garden", "patent-leather shoes", "flowers", "volatility of tissue paper", "japanned boxes". His painting now aimed to allow the modification of structures by a process he called "sconcertazione degli stati d'animo" ("de-concerting" or "breaking down" a "state of mind"). Here was a recapitulation of all his work on the themes of speed, light, theatre, decoration, on naturalistic and psychological approaches. After so much analysis, this remarkable series represented the moment of synthesis.

Bragaglia, who organized the exhibition, spoke of a "mental vision" superimposing itself on the artist's physical eye. He concluded: "Looking at the same landscape, Balla has influenced it with different colours and distortions suggested by his mental vision." One need only imagine all these paintings together to understand the novelty of the experiment: the same drawing with different colours each time, the same image with infinite variations. Starting from nature he reaches abstraction, but always in a form enriched by experiences made along the way. In other words, abstraction means starting from nature, leaving it behind and then inevitably coming back to it. And when the painter has discovered his own mental formula, perfect as rock-crystal, the scheme can be enriched by a natural sensation ("evening") or a pictorial effect ("amethyst"). Mood, in Pirandello-like fashion, gives research a two-fold aspect in the metaphysical mystery of "naked masks".

Tempera on paper, 94 × 107 (37 × 42⅛).
Signed below left: FUTUR BALLA. On the back: PAESAGGIO BALLA 1913.
Provenance: Casa Balla; Kouros Gallery, New York.
Exhibitions: Roma, 1959-60 (label on back); Torino, 1963, no. 115; Basel, 1982, p. 27; Wien, 1985, no. 16; Zürich, 1985, no. 14; New York, 1986, no. 17; Vancouver, 1986, no. 8.
Bibliography: *Archivi del Futurismo*, 1962, no. 59; Lista, 1982, no. 378.

Vortice + spazio (Vortex + Space), c. 1914.

Linea di velocità + vortice (Speed-line + Vortex), 1913. Oil on canvas. Private collection.

Ponte della velocità (Bridge of Speed), c. 1913. Oil and collage on paste-board. Galleria Nazionale d'Arte Moderna, Roma (Balla Bequest).

In 1913 his research again came to a stop and then restarted, just as had happened in 1912 when he shifted from the analysis of relative motion to absolute motion. Different stages of research succeeded one another within a very short space of time, like waves in a controlled tide.

With his "Vortices", in a certain sense Balla started again from scratch. After achieving the "line of speed", he experimented with another "force-form" that could lead him into the mysteries of the sky. He produced studies as precise as technical diagrams (such as the work analyzed here), but also pure painterly compositions like the canvas dated 1913 reproduced above.

As soon as he discovered his force-form, he identified new fields to be explored with it. His extraordinary *Bridge of Speed* (*Ponte della velocità*) — the more complex of the two versions is reproduced here — presents real architecture in a science-fiction atmosphere. The metallic springiness of the vortex recalls the great tower designed by Tatlin a few years later in revolutionary Russia.

Charcoal on paper, 41 × 61 (16¹/₈ × 24).
Signed lower left: FUTUR BALLA (stamped with the "Pugno di Boccioni").
Provenance: Casa Balla; private collection, Milano.
Exhibitions: Torino, 1963, no. 100; Wien, 1985, no. 17; Zürich, 1985, no. 13; New York, 1986, no. 16.
Bibliography: *Archivi del Futurismo*, 1962, no. 107; Lista, 1982, no. 347.

Vortice + spazio + forme volume (*Vortex + Space + Volume Forms*), c. 1914.

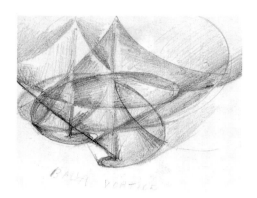

Vortice (*Vortex*), 1914. Charcoal on invitation card for the 1911 Rome exhibition. Private collection.

Svolversvulvortice, 1914. Charcoal on paper. Private collection.

Vortice (*Vortex*), c. 1914. Enamels on paper. Private collection.

A whole notebook (no. 3) was devoted to a study of the "Vortex" in a series of realistically abstract sketches. After the discovery of celestial orbits — experimented in *Densities of Atmosphere* (*Spessori di atmosfera*), 1913 — Balla looked for a form that would provide a dynamic link between earth and sky. The vortex does exist in nature but is chiefly visible to the mental eye. Its definition led Balla from his analysis of the dynamic forces on earth (car, line of speed) to an analysis of the dynamic forces of the sky (from solar eclipses to spiritistic transformations).

The painting considered here, an authoritative version dating from 1914, combines the form of the vortex with the volume-forms of space. The great painter seems to be trying to break out of the canvas, bringing to mind Boccioni's phrase, "The picture will no longer hold us." Around the same time Balla created a multi-material sculpture on precisely this subject. It was published in the manifesto *The Futurist Reconstruction of the Universe*, launched in March 1915 by Balla and his pupil Fortunato Depero (this document was to become

a source for the work of the Russian Constructivists).

The manifesto explains the need for his new exploration: "Balla began by studying the speed of automobiles and discovered its laws and essential force-lines. After more than twenty paintings devoted to this exploration, he understood that the single plane of the canvas did not allow the dynamic volume of speed to be rendered in depth. Balla felt the need to build the first dynamic plastic ensemble using wire, card-board sheets, fabrics, tissue-paper etc."

Oil on canvas, 75 × 97 (29$^1/_2$ × 38$^1/_4$).
Signed lower left: BALLA. On the back: VORTICE + SPAZIO + FORME VOLUME.
Provenance: Casa Balla, no. 14; Kouros Gallery, New York.
Exhibitions: Basel, 1982, p. 31; Wien, 1985, no. 19; Zürich, 1985, no. 20; New York, 1986, no. 24; Vancouver, 1986, no. 10.
Bibliography: Fagiolo, 1968 (1970, part III), no. 15; Lista, 1982, no. 389.

Mercurio passa davanti al sole (*Mercury Passing in Front of the Sun*), study, c. 1914.

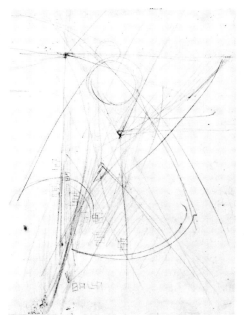

Mercurio che passa davanti al sole (*Mercury Passing in Front of the Sun*), study, c. 1914. Pencil on paper. Private collection.

Mercurio che passa davanti al sole (*Mercury Passing in Front of the Sun*), study, c. 1914. Charcoal on paper. The Museum of Modern Art, New York.

Spessori di spazio (*Densities of Space*), c. 1913. Pencil on paste-board. Private collection.

7 November 1914: the planet Mercury passed in front of the Sun. Over a few months Balla (who had observed the event with his telescope) painted a series of canvases on the subject (a dozen works including sketches, designs and syntheses).

As usual the starting point was absolutely real; the end result was in a sense surreal. In the centre we see the dark conical shape of the telescope, the main structural element of the composition. Above is the Sun and against it the tiny form of Mercury

observed through a smoked glass. Halfway down there is a "densities of atmosphere" effect, and to the left a zig-zagging movement of light (the refraction of the sun in an eye looking outside the telescope). The starting point is positivist. Rather than being reconstructed intellectually, light is surprised and studied at the moment when it appears as a natural phenomenon. This was exactly the procedure Balla had used for the sunsets and night-scenes of his early period, and for the rainbows of the "Interpenetrations". So here again the artist is not interested in the mysticism of nature, but in its religiousness: pantheism, or perhaps panpsychism.

Pencil on paper, 34.5 × 27 (13⅝ × 10⅝).
Signed lower right: BALLA (stamped with the "Pugno di Boccioni").
Provenance: Casa Balla, no. 34.
Exhibitions: Torino, 1963, no. 113.
Bibliography: *Archivi del Futurismo*, 1962, no. 146.

Mercurio passa davanti al sole visto nel cannocchiale (Mercury Passing in Front of the Sun Seen through a Telescope), 1914.

Orbite celesti (Celestial Orbits), c. 1914. Oil on canvas. Private collection.

Balla had already explored the subject of the sky. In his early period he had painted a large canvas (lost, known from photographs of his studio) entitled *The Constellation of Orion (La costellazione di Orione)*. Its only subject is the night sky seen from his balcony, faintly marked by astral lights. In his Futurist period he painted *Celestial Orbits (Orbite celesti)*, reproduced here, and *Densities of Atmosphere (Spessori d'atmosfera)*, the masterpiece which was lost after the 1914 exhibition in London.

His notebooks often include studies for "densities of air" and "dust motes". As for Mercury, a reproduction is entitled *Densities of Atmosphere + Telescope*, while in a drawing the theme seems to have expanded (as usual) because the title reads *Interpenetration of the Self with the Universe (Compenetrazione dell'io con l'universo)*.

It is interesting to note how Balla's search for "equivalents" of the secret planetary harmonies resurfaces in later studies, either real (a flying aeroplane) or purely imaginary (the series of "Forms-Spirits Transformations").

Mixed media (pastel, tempera, oil) on paper, 82.7 × 60 (32⅝ × 23⅝).
Signed lower left: BALLA 1914.
Provenance: Casa Balla, no. 63.
Exhibitions: Vancouver, 1986, no. 12.

Bottiglia × spazio (Bottle × Space), c. 1914.

Umberto Boccioni, *Forme-forza di una bottiglia (Force-forms of a Bottle)*, c. 1913. After an old photograph (by courtesy of Giuseppe Sprovieri).

Sculpture to Balla was not a new technique to be experimented with, but a necessary outcome of his research. In his notebooks we often find studies for sculptures he never made. The design here, on the other hand, seems to echo the ideas of his friend and ex-pupil Boccioni, whose explosive sculptures Balla had seen in Milan in 1913.

The manifesto on sculpture which followed soon after this project announced the aim of a volatile, even kinetic sculpture. Balla's ideas for a "Futurist reconstruction of the universe" are curiously close to the "Constructivism" proclaimed as a doctrine a few years later by the Russians. A passage from the manifesto signed by Gabo and Pevsner reads: "You sculptors of every shadow and relief still cling to the centuries-old prejudice that volume cannot be freed from mass. We reject the ancient artistic illusion that static rhythms are the only components of the plastic arts. We claim that in these arts there exists the new element of kinetic rhythms, as basic forms of our perception of real time."

Coloured crayons on paper, 58.5 × 41 (23 × 16¹⁄₈).
Signed lower left: FUTUR BALLA (stamped with the "Pugno di Boccioni").
Provenance: Casa Balla.
Exhibitions: Roma, 1971, no. 36; Roma, 1971- 72, no. 46; Zürich, 1985, no. 23; New York, 1986, no. 27.
Bibliography: Lista, 1982, no. 375.

Complesso plastico di frastuono + velocità (Plastic Ensemble of Din + Speed), 1914.

Complesso plastico colorato di frastuono + danza + allegria - specchi, stagnole, talco, cartone, filferro (Plastic Ensemble Coloured with Din + Dance + Gaiety - mirrors, tinfoils, talc, cardboard, wire), c. 1914. Original photograph of one of the "Plastic Ensembles" presented in the manifesto *Futurist Reconstruction of the Universe*, 11 March 1915.

Complesso plastico colorato di frastuono + velocità - cartone e stagnole colorate (Plastic Ensemble Coloured with Din + Speed - cardboard and coloured tinfoils), c. 1914. Original photograph of one of the "Plastic Ensembles" presented in the manifesto *Futurist Reconstruction of the Universe*, 11 March 1915.

The manifesto *The Futurist Reconstruction of the Universe*, signed by Balla together with Depero (11 March 1915), provides the prehistory of the "Plastic Ensembles". These were a form of sculpture peculiar to Balla, made with perishable materials which had all the fascination of the ephemeral (also experimented by Boccioni in sculptures of the human body and imagined by Sant'Elia for the houses of the future).

A few old photographs have preserved the memory of those fantastic aggregations of forms. In Balla's notebooks there are valuable jottings and ideas, together with the addresses of the most advanced sculptors of the time, Archipenko and Alexandra Exter.

It was obvious that Balla would have to venture into the field of sculpture to explore "form-lines" (going beyond Boccioni's "force-lines"). The fact that he called himself a "Futurist Abstractionist", however, indicated the direction and novelty of his experiments.

In his manifesto we read: "So art becomes a Presence, a new Object, a new reality created with the abstract elements of the universe. The hands of the traditionalist artists suffered from the loss of the Object.

Our hands are eager to find a new Object to be created."

In at least three "Plastic Ensembles" Balla combined movement and light in an atmosphere of "miracles and magic", leaving one of his most suggestive and subtle ideas to the later avant-garde.

These sculptures, made with perishable materials, were taken up again by Balla during the Second World War. With his blacksmith friend Armando Ricci, who had a forge in Via Oslavia, first in 1940 and then again in 1955 (when Balla was rediscovered), the artist designed a few of variants of these sculptures, this time made to last.

Originally made of perishable materials. Platinized steel plates mounted on wood, 51 × 59 × 10 (20⅛ × 23¼ × 4).
Provenance: Casa Balla.
Exhibitions: Torino, 1963, no. 233; Wien, 1985, no. 21; Zürich, 1985, no. 21; New York, 1986, no. 25; Vancouver, 1986, no. 2.
Bibliography: Crispolti, 1962; Calvesi, 1967, p. 41; Fagiolo, 1968 (1970, part III), pp. 70-75.

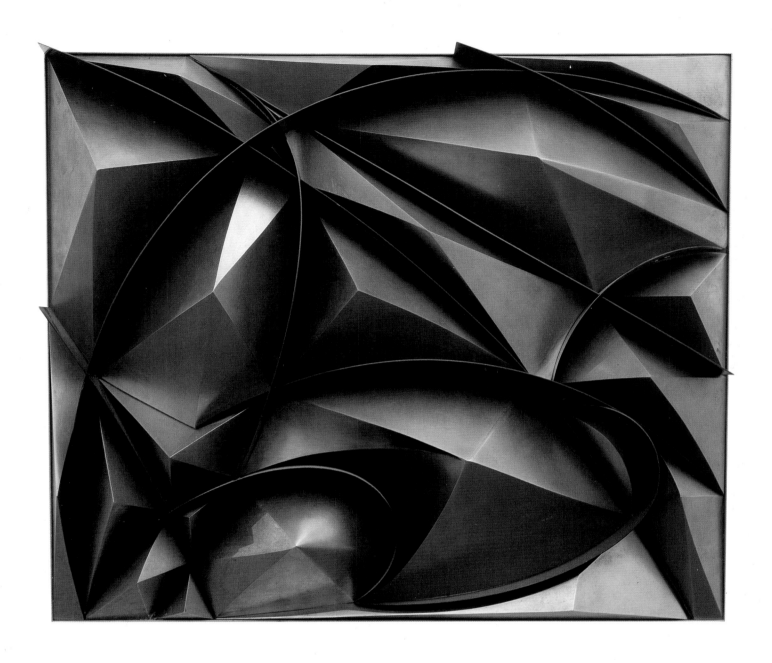

Forze aeroplano Caproni (*Caproni Aeroplane Forces*), c. 1915.

Linee di forza di aeroplano Caproni (*Caproni Aeroplane Force-lines*), c. 1915. Pastels on paper. Private collection.

The "Vorticism" manifesto signed by Ezra Pound, published in the magazine *Blast*, London, 1914.

After the "Futurist" theme of cars, he tackled the "futuristic" subject of the Caproni aeroplane, one of the large, clumsy heroes of the First World War (Giuseppe Sprovieri closed his Futurist galleries in Rome and Naples to fly a Caproni in D'Annunzio's squadron). This is a painting influenced by the wartime mood, a search for "equivalents" between machine forms and nature.

Once again Balla started from an objective study, documented in his notebooks, this time on a turning propeller. His "abstract" equivalent was not very different from his solution for car wheels. In February 1914 in Sprovieri's Rome gallery he exhibited a painting entitled *Densities of Air + Dynamism of Helix* (*Spessori d'aria + dinamismo d'elica*).

The historic avant-garde was interested in the new reality of aeroplanes. In particular Vorticism, the movement formed in London round the poet Ezra Pound and artist Wyndham Lewis, appreciated the idea of dynamism.

Charcoal on paper, 30 × 41 (11⁷/₈ × 16¹/₈).
Signed lower right: FUTUR BALLA.
Provenance: Casa Balla, no. 374; private collection, Torino.
Bibliography: Lista, 1984, no. 1103.

Bandiere all'Altare della Patria (Flags at the National Altar), 1915.

Forme-volume del grido "Viva l'Italia" (Volume-forms of the Cry "Viva l'Italia"),
1915. Oil on canvas. Galleria Nazionale d'Arte Moderna, Roma (Balla
Bequest).

Le insidie del 9 maggio (Insidie di guerra) (The Risks of 9 May - Risks of War),
1915. Oil on canvas. Galleria Nazionale d'Arte Moderna, Roma (Balla
Bequest).

Like the other Futurists, Balla was enthusiastic about "interventionism", Italian participation in the war. His large oils of this period (exhibited as a complete set by Bragaglia in 1918) and his intense sketches — about fifteen works altogether — show his desire to channel the preceding analytical studies into a grandiose portrayal of states of mind.

Boccioni's reaction was remarkable. He wrote to Balla from the front, "My very dear and great friend! I loved your paintings! You are great! Bravo, my very dear friend! But I wasn't surprised — you are capable of any miracle of genius and willpower! Bravo again, and best wishes for your work!"

And in September 1918 Boccioni wrote in *Gli Avvenienti*: "Over a few months Balla has passed through a very rapid evolution. His latest works, inspired by the violent anti-neutralist rallies, have reached results probably unequalled in Europe today. There is no longer just one objective plastic value — everything is transfigured by the idea of dynamism, interpreted through an intuitive sense of abstraction. All that could be considered episodic or contingent has been ruthlessly eliminated, with an iron conviction that is almost frightening. Any irregularity could lead him to deviate from the dogma he believes in and which he has taken to its extreme consequences. Anything that appears to him weakness is abolished. He goes on destroying. The earth becomes majolica-crystal. Iron becomes polished steel. The tree is replaced by glossy walnut. The paint has given up the irregularities of Romanticism and become enamel. An enamelled surface seems to him warmer than blood that flows and spurts irregularly. Steel and crystal. We have achieved absolute purity."

Coming back to the paintings, a number of them are brilliantly coloured. In *Waving Flags + Crowd (Sbandieramento + folla)* the violet spirals of the crowd of demonstrators are intensified by the tri-coloured "fireworks" (the red, white and green of the Italian flag) and transmitted to the sky. In others the subdued, dramatic tints exemplify the relationship between colour and states of mind that will be the subject of *Pessimism and Optimism (Pessimismo e ottimismo)*, 1923.

Frame painted by the artist.
Oil on canvas, 30 × 31.2 (11⁷/₈ × 12¹/₄).
Signed lower right: FUTUR BALLA.
Provenance: Casa Balla; private collection, Milano.
Exhibitions: Roma, 1986, no. 3; New York, 1986, no. 29; Venezia, 1986a, no. 3.
Bibliography: Lista, 1982, no. 442.

Il pugno di Boccioni (*Boccioni's Fist*), study a, c. 1915.

Red crayon on paper, 10 × 15 (4 × 5⁷/₈).
Provenance: Casa Balla, no. 411; private collection, Milano.
Exhibitions: Torino, 1963, no. 240; New York, 1985, p. 20.
Bibliography: Fagiolo, 1968 (1970, part III), no. 36; Calvesi, 1967, p. 15; Lista, 1982, no. 453.

Il pugno di Boccioni (*Boccioni's Fist*), study b, c. 1915.

Red crayon on paper, 10 × 13 (4 × 5¹/₈).
Provenance: Casa Balla, no. 411; private collection, Milano.
Exhibitions: Torino, 1963, no. 239; New York, 1985, p. 20.
Bibliography: Fagiolo, 1968 (1970, part III), no. 35; Calvesi, 1967, p. 15; Lista, 1982, no. 454.

Il pugno di Boccioni (*Boccioni's Fist*),
study c, c. 1915.

Pencil on paper, 10 × 14 (4 × 5¹/₂).
Signed lower right: BALLA.
Provenance: Casa Balla, no. 411; private collection, Milano.
Exhibitions: Torino, 1963, no. 241; New York,
1985, p. 18.
Bibliography: *Archivi del Futurismo*, 1962, no.
223; Fagiolo, 1968 (1970, part III), no. 34; Calvesi, 1967, p. 15; Lista, 1982, no. 449.

Il pugno di Boccioni (*Boccioni's Fist*),
study d, c. 1915.

Pencil on paper, 13.6 × 19.5 (5³/₈ × 7³/₄).
Signed lower left: BALLA.
Provenance: Casa Balla, no. 411; private collection, Milano.
Exhibitions: Torino, 1963, no. 238; New York,
1985, p. 21.
Bibliography: *Archivi del Futurismo*, 1962, no.
226; Calvesi, 1967, p. 15; Fagiolo, 1968 (1970,
part III), no. 37; Lista, 1982, no. 451.

Il pugno di Boccioni (Boccioni's Fist), c. 1915.

Futurismo contro Passatismo (Futurism versus Passéism), c. 1915. Pencil on paper. Private collection.

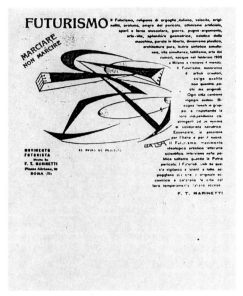

The "Pugno di Boccioni" ("Boccioni's Fist") used for the letter-head of the Futurist Movement.

Balla in Boccioni's studio in 1913 in front of the sculpture *Forme uniche di continuità nello spazio* (*Unique Forms of Continuity in Space*): at the back, Boccioni: in the foreground, his mother.

Balla seemed to return to "representation" in a form close to Boccioni's, but always with his own unmistakeable abstract tendency. His *Force-lines of Boccioni's Fist* (*Linee di forza del pugno di Boccioni*) dates from 1915; a version made of cardboard and red wood is now in the Winston collection (Birmingham, USA). His need to break away from the plane of the paper can be felt in all the many studies that were subsequently catalyzed in this aggressive spatial image. Boccioni's fist, a design which reappeared on the Futurist move-ment's letter-paper, has a figurative and also a symbolical meaning. In the drawing reproduced above, Futurism attacks Pas-séism, a decrepit old man among columns and arches (this reading is plainly inscrib-ed on one of the first drawings, over a tangle of dynamic lines).

As we see from other drawings, Balla was determined to achieve a synthetic dynamic image. The running figure is placed on a schematized mountain ("We Futurists are climbing up to the highest and most radiant peaks and we proclaim ourselves the Lords of light," announced the *Futurist Technical Manifesto*). Starting from a dynamic break-down (of the sort used for the dog or the violinist) he reaches a synthesis of formal violence.

Study related to the poster for the Casa d'Arte Bragaglia.
Watercolour on paper, 13.5 × 20 (5½ × 7⅞).
Signed lower right: BALLA FUTURISTA.
Provenance: Casa Balla, no. 411; private collection, Milano.
Exhibitions: Torino, 1963, no. 237; New York, 1985, p. 19.
Bibliography: Calvesi, 1967, p. 15; Fagiolo, 1968 (1970, part III), no. 38; Lista, 1982, no. 456.

Il pugno di Boccioni (*Boccioni's Fist*), cartoon, c. 1915.

Balla holding up the red-painted cardboard sculpture *Linee forza del pugno di Boccioni* (*Force-lines of Boccioni's Fist*): in the background, Futurist flowers on a painted screen. Photograph taken around 1930.

This extraordinary work is the outcome of his studies, an executive cartoon of the sort the Old Masters made, but in this case prepared for a modern sculpture. The idea of the forms is defined, the dynamic forces evoked by the figure are indicated, and the colour is specified (red, as in all revolutionary ideas).

The primary idea is not to destroy but to construct, or rather re-construct (the universe). This was also to be the vision of Soviet Constructivism. It is interesting to re-read the manifesto launched by Gabo and Pevsner in August 1920. The sustained attack upon Futurism tells us where their sources are: "With plumb-line in hand, with the infallible eyes of conquerors, with compass-precision minds, we build our work as the universe shapes its own."

Other writings by Gabo (the real theorist) confirm that he was familiar with the *Futurist Reconstruction of the Universe*. A passage in his essay *The Idea of Constructivist Realism* reads: "What we call 'acquiring knowledge' is nothing but the acquisition of the ability to construct and improve the gigantic jigsaw-puzzle of images which together represent, and for us are, the universe. What our knowledge leads us to discover is not something different from ourselves, a particle of superior reality, permanent and absolute, just waiting to be understood. We can only discover our own contribution. Electricity, rays, the atom, the thousand other facts that we think we have discovered, in reality have been made by us. They are images we have constructed."

As for the works, it was only around 1917 that Gabo and Pevsner managed to break away from their initial Cubism and turn towards structures of the sort made by Balla.

Coloured inks on paper, 114 × 101.5 (44⁷/₈ × 40).
Signed upper right: FUTUR BALLA.
Provenance: Casa Balla, no. 652.
Exhibitions: Roma, 1959 (label on back).
Bibliography: *Archivi del Futurismo*, 1962, no. 226b (not reproduced); Fagiolo, 1968 (1970, part III), no. 47; Lista, 1982, no. 457.

Corazzata + vedova + vento (Battleship + Widow + Wind), 1916.

Dimostrazione interventista (Interventionist Rally), c. 1915. Oil and collage on paper. Private collection.

The artist's daughters confirm that Balla considered this painting one of his most important achievements along the path of "states of mind" and abstraction. He exhibited it for the first time at the Casa d'Arte Bragaglia in 1918 with the title I

have given — rather than the usual *Widow's Veil + Landscape (Velo di vedova + paesaggio)*. His aim was to add together three elements: an idea of dynamic nature (wind), that of a person and her state of mind (widow), and a war machine (the battleship). A few months later the painting was shown again, in the large Milan exhibition in Palazzo Cova which seems to have marked the arrival-point (and end?) of Futurism. Here the painting received a new but still synthetic title: *Landscape + Mourning + Battleship (Paesaggio + lutto + corazzata)*.

The painting was published by Christian Zervos when studies of Futurism started again after the war, and subsequently had a long history of exhibitions and international changes of ownership.

Balla's aim is reconfirmed as a determination to represent the unrepresentable (the force of wind, in this case) by means of "abstract equivalents". The colour corresponds to both the state of mind (the ancient dark blue of melancholy) and the ob-

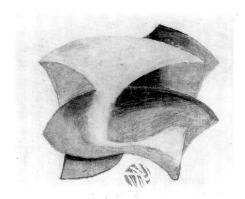

Study of a tree for the painting *Velo di vedova + paesaggio (Widow's Veil + Landscape)*, c. 1916. Pencil on paper. Private collection.

jective requirements of representation (the grey-green of the battleship). The conclusion is that is possible to portray a widow and her memory of a handsome sailor with his instrument of war tossed by the wind, without showing a single figure.

Frame painted by the artist.
Oil on canvas, 105 × 110 (41³/₈ × 43¹/₄).
Signed lower left: BALLA 1916.
Provenance: Casa Balla; Costantino Marino, Milano; Galleria Daverio, Milano; private collection, London.
Exhibitions: Roma, 1918, no. 21; Milano, 1919, no. 18 (*Paesaggio + lutto + corazzata*); New York (Rose Fried), 1954, no. 14; Zürich, 1950; Torino, 1963, no. 136; Milano, 1980, no. 4.
Bibliography: Zervos, 1950, p. 69; *Archivi del Futurismo*, 1962, no. 193; Barricelli, 1967, no. 50; Crispolti, 1975, no. 21; Lista, 1982, no. 506.

119

Alberi mutilati (*Mutilated Trees*), study, c. 1918.

Alberi mutilati (*Mutilated Trees*), 1918. Oil on canvas. Private collection.

The canvas *Mutilated Trees* (*Alberi mutilati* or *Taglio del bosco*), reproduced here was painted at the same time as *Battleship + Widow + Landscape* (*Corazzata + vedova + paesaggio*), or at least reflects the same state of mind. It was considered very important by the artist, as its history shows. In 1920 it was shown at the Geneva exhibition which marked the first "rentrée" of the Italians in Europe; in 1926 it was sent to New York and Boston; and it was also presented in two retrospective shows of Balla's work (the 1925 Rome Biennial; a room at the Amatori e Cultori in 1928). His return to landscape was complicated by the wartime mood, resulting in a work which is at the same time symbolic and dramatic. The best interpretation has been given by his daughter Elica (in her book *Con Balla*, Milano, 1984): "With the dramatic sensations of the war still impressed on his feelings, the artist who loved nature experienced the amputated branches of his beloved trees like the amputation of limbs. The sections of the cut branches stand out small and luminous from the gloomy shadows of the wood. From the point of the cut, force-lines depart and run into the mass of dark greens of the undergrowth, dominated by the sinister gleam of the wounding blade. The forest experiences the same pain as the heart of the artist who looks and feels. We hear the thud of the falling trunks and see the aching wounds of the great mutilated tree. The colours are few: green, black and white, with an overtone of violet shadow."

Pastel on paste-board, 45.5 × 33.6 (18 × 13¼).
Provenance: Casa Balla, no. 123.
Exhibitions: Basel, 1982, p. 42 and appendix; Wien, 1985, no. 25; Zürich, 1985, no. 30; New York, 1986, no. 35.
Bibliography: *Archivi del Futurismo*, 1962, no. 264a.

Paesaggio + volo di rondini (Landscape + Swifts' Flight), 1918.

Volo di rondini (Swifts' Flight), 1913. Tempera on paper. Formerly A. Barr Jr. collection, New York.

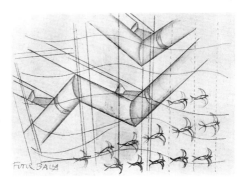

Volo di rondini (Swifts' Flight), study, c. 1913. Inks on paper. Private collection.

Volo di rondini (Swifts' Flight), 1913. Tempera on paper. Private collection.

In the harmonious moment when he rediscovered landscape, almost naturally Balla also returned to one of his first experimental themes, swifts. Initially he made simple studies of the shorthand of flight, subsequently complicated by a placing in space. The most complex painting of the series is *Lines of Directions + Dynamic Successions (Linee andamentali + successioni dinamiche)* — reproduced here is a simplified version. The subject is flight in its "Dynamic Successions", overlaid by a few static realities (the guttering, a shutter). These are set in motion by winding luminous lines indicating the artist's movement along the terrace as he observes the birds' flight. The fusion between movement, trajectory of his own spirit and the real setting (his ex-monastery home in Via Paisiello) creates a synthetic "line of force". And finally, since this is an "abstract" representation, the definitive title of the painting (shown in Florence in 1914 and published in Boccioni's *Pittura scultura futuriste*) does not mention the swifts, which were the starting point of the exploration. The final result is a complex synthesis of light, movement, space, mood, objectivity and psychology.

In this canvas from 1918 his intense analytical research seems to have been forgotten. Its place is taken by a stronger decorative impulse, creating an "expansion" of forms and colours which was to have a great influence on a new Futurist generation composed of increasingly weak followers.

Watercolour on paper, 38.5 × 64.5 (15^{1}/$_{8}$ × 25^{3}/$_{8}$).
Signed lower left: FUTUR BALLA 1918.
Provenance: Casa Balla; private collection, Milano.
Exhibitions: Newcastle-Edinburgh, 1971-72 (labels on back).
Bibliography: *Archivi del Futurismo*, 1962, n. 291t (not reproduced); Lista, 1982, no. 633.

Futurlibecciata (*Futur South-westerly Gale*), c. 1919.

Marvelante (arazzo dipinto)   BALLA   Voiles sur la mer (tapisserie peinte)

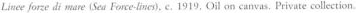

Linee forze di mare (*Sea Force-lines*), c. 1919. Oil on canvas. Private collection.

Marvelante (*Seasailing*), painted tapestry, c. 1924. Drawing from the magazine *Noi* edited by Enrico Prampolini, for the tapestry shown at the "Art Déco" exhibition, Paris, 1925.

This work is part of a series of studies and paintings (about twenty altogether) which Balla started in Viareggio where he went for a short holiday in the summer of 1919. After the exhibition at Bragaglia's in autumn, he had been to Milan for the great Futurist show at Palazzo Cova where he exhibited fourteen works. One of the psychological reasons for his return to the force-forms of nature may have been the sight of that array of post-Futurists applying his discoveries in a very uninspired fashion.

As always, starting from the image of sea-sky-sails, Balla analyses various subjects. He adds to the theme the feeling of night (*Seashadow - Marombra*), he breaks it up into its equivalents (*Sea Force-lines - Linee forza di mare*), he studies the horizon line and the rhythms of boats and sky, which by empathy suggest those of the sea (*Sea + Sky + Sails - Mare + cielo + vele*). Or, as in the case of the work presented here, he analyses the effect of the wind which adds further dynamism to elements already dynamic in themselves. And finally, he takes the representation to an abstract synthesis.

The frame in the shape of lashing waves added to a number of paintings in the series emphasizes the direction of his research, which is dynamic and at the same time decorative — a cypher of dynamism. The pictorial quality, with smooth surfaces and well-defined forms, anticipates Art Déco. Not by chance the 1925 exhibition in Paris included Balla's tapestry-picture with sea and sails (on this page appears a synthetic drawing of the work, published by Balla in Prampolini's magazine *Noi*).

Oil on canvas, 80 × 100 (31$^{1/2}$ × 39$^{3/8}$).
Original shaped and painted frame.
Signed lower right: BALLA. On the back of the canvas: FUTUR LIBECCIATA BALLA.
Provenance: Casa Balla.
Exhibitions: Vancouver, 1986, no. 21.
Bibliography: *Archivi del Futurismo*, 1962, no. 317m (not reproduced); Lista, 1982, no. 648.

Sorge l'idea (The Idea Rises), c. 1920.

Morbidezze di primavera (Softnesses of Spring), 1916. Pencil on paper. Private collection.

Dissolvimento d'autunno (Autumn Dissolution), c. 1918. Oil on canvas. Private collection.

Forze estive (Summer Forces), c. 1918. Oil on canvas. Private collection.

After the war Balla seemed to pause to reconsider all the motifs and "variations on a theme" he had developed over the past ten years. It was like a moment of reflection before starting afresh. His work done at the end of the war combined abstraction and symbolism. In this canvas, for example, the Idea becomes a throbbing centrepoint generating forms and colour that invite a comparison with nature.

Already at the end of 1918 his friend Bragaglia showed Balla's experiments on the subject of the seasons (a *Spring* had appeared in the dancer Massine's collection in early 1917). The various different moments (see the reproductions here) go from *Softnesses of Spring* (*Morbidezze di primavera*) to *Dissolution of Autumn* (*Dissolvimento di autunno*) and *Summer Forces* (*Forze estive*).

Balla had looked for dynamism in his "thought forms", deducing it from accidental events (a car, a telescope, an aeroplane). Now he rediscovered it simply in the eternal cycle of nature.

Oil on wood, 35.8 × 28.6 (14¹/₈ × 11¹/₄).
Signed below: FUTUR BALLA.
Provenance: Casa Balla; Antonio Mazzotta, Milano.
Exhibitions: Frankfurt, 1963, no. 7.

Ballerine del Bal Tik Tak (Dancers at the Bal Tik Tak), c. 1921.

This swirling image is connected to Balla's designs for a cabaret which opened in Rome in 1921, at a time when he was still fascinated by the idea of Futurist dynamism. The ballerina, broken down into her aerial rhythms, seems to echo the idea of "unanimity" proclaimed by his ex-pupil (and friend) Gino Severini.

The French paper *Les Tablettes* published a report under the heading "A Futurist Inauguration", signed by C. Caillot: "The very walls seem to dance: great architectural lines interpenetrate in strong colours, light and very dark blues... An enormous green clover-leaf club distorts the lines of a diamond and a pine-cone spade, or cuts a yellow heart, as though gigantic animated playing cards were being shuffled. A dancer with a fan breaks down her movements; tricoloured pillars are as welcoming as a convivial 14 July. The spiral staircase has beautiful yellow and red harmonies and leads to the temptations of a joyous hell."

Study for the sign with moving lights made for the *Bal Tik Tak* in 1921. Watercolour on paper.

Pencil on paper, 48 × 56 (18⁷/₈ × 22).
Signed lower left: FUTUR BALLA.
Provenance: Casa Balla.

Scienza contro oscurantismo (Science versus Obscurantism), 1920.

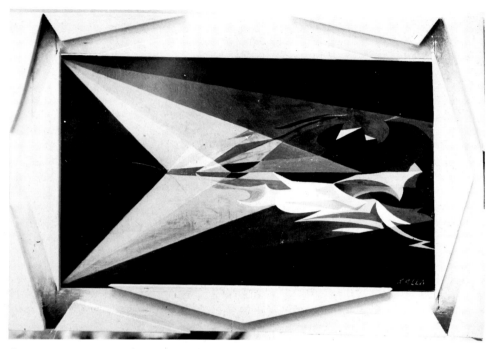

Oscurantismo e progresso (*Obscurantism and Progress*), 1920. Frame carved by the artist. Oil on wood. Private collection.

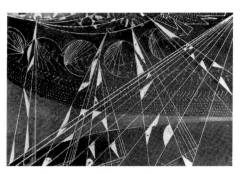

Trasformazione forme spiriti (*Forms-Spirits Transformation*), c. 1918. Watercolour on paper. Private collection.

Now Balla started to go deeper into the symbolism of clashing forces, which had always interested him. Forms and colours were opposed: light/dark, soft/sharp, earth/sky. And new themes appeared, always in a key of *Einfühlung*, that hard-to-translate German concept that Balla was very familiar with and rendered with various adjectives (*Numbers Sympathizing - Numeri simpatizzanti*; *Numbers in Love - Numeri innamorati*). This was the image of his state of mind, which became increasingly clear (a 1919 collage is entitled *Plastic Values -* *Valori Plastici*). And so his new paintings were called *Science against Obscurantism* (*Scienza contro Oscurantismo*), *Obscurantism and Progress* (*Oscurantismo e progresso*) *Pessimism and Optimism* (*Pessimismo e ottimismo*).

This path ultimately led him to take an interest in voices from the beyond, in a dozen works — one is reproduced here — dedicated to spiritism (it should be remembered that Boccioni also mentions his experiments with a medium). Departing from the earth's curvature, the triangles which have always signified spirituality rise to touch a sky in which the stars create a harmonious clash between forms and forces. *Forms and Thought - Spiritic Vision* (*Forme e pensiero - visione spiritica*) is the title of one of these paintings, exhibited at Bragaglia's gallery. Even hermetic and paranormal perceptions were given a Futurist form.

Balla wrote about himself: "His is a strange character, a *temperamentino* (as he himself would say) which gets on much better with the voices of the infinite than our own." In fact his parascientific interests — Röntgen rays, astronomy, alchemy, hermeticism, the study of mysteries — were not a final flourish of his poetic vision but the very foundations of his work as an artist. He was always something of a magician, a witch-doctor, an alchemist.

Whenever he needed to find the answer to an accumulation of questions, in other words identify a provisional synthesis after exhausting analysis, Balla would again lift his eyes to the sky.

Tempera on paste-board, 28.6 × 39.5 (11¼ × 15½).
Signed lower right: FUTUR BALLA. On the back: SCIENZA CONTRO OSCURANTISMO 1920 BALLA (stamped with the "Pugno di Boccioni").
Provenance: Casa Balla; Marella Agnelli, Torino (inscription on back).

131

Numeri innamorati (*Numbers in Love*), c. 1920.

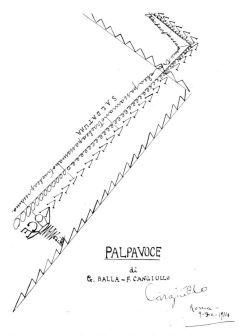

The first example of "words in freedom". *Palpavoce* by Balla and Cangiullo, 1914. Ink on paper. Private collection.

The theory of empathy (*Einfühlung*) is another of the heritages of the symbolist and secessionist movement which Balla was to take with him in his life as an artist. The originality of this work lies in harmonizing recognizable forms and a picture which in its way is abstract. The figures become solid characters, while the colour alludes to an interpenetration (yellow and blue create light blue).

Other (hermetic) meanings may be sought in these numbers which simultaneously approach and withdraw from one another. Reviewing the exhibition, his pupil Enrico Prampolini wrote that in *Numbers in Love*, Balla "has discovered the new perspective sympathies and architectural constructions that an arabesque of numbers can suggest."

Balla always considered numbers and letters as images. In his pre-war Futurist period, he was among the first to experiment with the magic meaning of letters: in *Touchvoice* (*Palpavoce*), for example, he depicts a flight of steps with a hand touching the voice coming down the stair-

The word makes the picture. *Quando*, c. 1918. Tempera on paper. Private collection.

well, all represented using only the letters of the alphabet. In the 20s he created abstract paintings starting from a single word ("perhaps", "when") hermetically concealed in the colour contrasts.

Oil on canvas, 77 × 56 (30¼ × 22).
Below left: BALLA FUTURISTA.
Provenance: Prospero Guarini, Milano; Giorgio Franchetti, Roma.
Exhibitions: Venezia, 1926, no. 5; Bologna, 1927, no. 6; Venezia, 1986, p. 317.
Bibliography: Costantini, 1934, p. 199; *Archivi del Futurismo*, 1962, no. 343; Calvesi, 1967, p. 126; Fagiolo, 1970, p. 110, no. 71; De Marchis, 1977, p. 94; Lista, 1982, no. 687.

S'è rotto l'incanto (The Spell Is Broken), study, c. 1920.

Il T (The T), c. 1920. Oil on canvas with wooden letters. Whereabouts unknown.

Balla was very interested in numbers and letters with their quality of being symbolical and at the same time real. His first "words in freedom" designs were intended to stimulate the spectator's mind. He also shared the taste for destroying traditional representation that resulted in works by Marinetti and Cangiullo appearing on the walls of the Cabaret Voltaire for the inauguration of the Dada movement in 1917.

It was only logical that research into abstraction should lead to a study of the most abstract of abstract devices: words. Many of Balla's masterpieces depict nothing but brightly coloured words (significant as well, of course) or else striking, slogan-like phrases. Coins and banknotes are other forms of abstraction, but language is supreme. We all understand one another thanks to something abstract. This fact may be compared to the way a Persian carpet seems merely decorative in use, whereas in reality it contains invocations to Allah; a Japanese *makemono* may appear delightfully "informel", but in fact it sings the praises of nature or love. In other words, to the ignorant (and the blind) everything appears as abstract.

"Velvet silence, many-coloured words", reads a phrase in Balla's notebooks. In the Twenties the artist continued his experimentation, making letters, words or numbers the heroes of the picture. In *The Spell Is Broken (È rotto l'incanto)*, a pink apparition is "broken" by sharp blades; *Numbers in Love (I numeri innamorati)* presents a yellowish-green mechanical structure; the painting *The T (Il T)*, reproduced above, is based on numbers, letters and punctuation marks.

At the 1926 Venice Biennial, in a room lent by the Soviet Union, a number of these authoritative paintings were hung beside similar experiments by Pannaggi and Paladini, who had invented a "mechanical" art. Reviewing the exhibition, Balla's ex-pupil Prampolini concluded: "*The Spell Is Broken*, composed of volumes of rose-coloured optimism broken by the contrast of mechanical-crystalline elements, has exceptional emotional force. Here the enigma of the 'state of mind' has been solved in a new chromatic-constructive harmony."

Oil on canvas, 40 × 30 (15¾ × 11¾).
Signed lower left: FUTUR BALLA. On the back: S'È ROTTO L'INCANTO BALLA.
Provenance: Casa Balla, no. 186.
Exhibitions: Vancouver, 1986, no. 23.

Pessimismo e ottimismo (*Pessimism and Optimism*), study, c. 1923.

Forze nuove (*New Forces*). Oil on canvas. Galleria Nazionale d'Arte Moderna, Roma (Balla Bequest).

Le frecce della vita (*The Arrows of Life*), c. 1929. Oil on canvas. Private collection.

This masterpiece represents the development of a theme announced in the painting *New Forces* (*Forze nuove*), reproduced here.

Balla often depicted two opposing forces which could also hold a lesson (another aspect of his painting that should not be overlooked). Positive/negative, yes/no, black/colour are given a definitive shape in this canvas. Balla considered it one of the complete expressions of Futurism.

Compared with the version usually exhibited and reproduced, the *Pessimism and Optimism* (*Pessimismo e ottimismo*) presented here is more concentrated — the reduced format may have contributed towards this result. Balla showed the larger painting — almost a propaganda statement — at the 1925 Rome Biennial and in his room at the Amatori e Cultori in 1928, which presented a sort of summing-up of his whole life as a painter. The version shown here seems to be the final one from several points of view. The other is probably a dilated public image of the "state of mind".

Here the past has been effectively destroyed to make room for future construction. In a 1914 notebook (no. 5) Balla had written about the need "to enter the great domain of the plastic state of mind with new equivalent abstract forms". Now, after so many laborious studies, in *Pessimism and Optimism* all the mysteries of light and movement are integrated with the "state of mind". Balla knew that he was touching a "great domain" and it was quite natural that in canvases like this one his painting should become almost cosmic.

Collage and tempera on paper, 21.5 x 29 (8$^{1/2}$ x 11$^{3/8}$).
Signed lower right: FUTUR BALLA.
Provenance: Casa Balla; Maurizio Fagiolo, Roma.
Exhibitions: Zürich, 1985, no. 33; New York, 1986, no. 39.

137

Pessimismo e ottimismo (*Pessimism and Optimism*), c. 1923.

Oil on canvas, 80 × 104.7 (31$^{1}/_{2}$ × 41$^{1}/_{4}$).
Signed lower right: FUTUR BALLA. On the back: G. BALLA, N. 2. PESSIMISMO E OTTIMISMO.
Provenance: Casa Balla; Studio 2C, Roma.
Exhibitions: Verona, 1976, no. 53.
Bibliography: *Archivi del Futurismo*, 1962, no. 364b (not reproduced); Lista, 1982, no. 742.

Dinamismo andamentale (Directional Dynamism), c. 1923.

Dramma di paesaggio (Landscape drama), c. 1918. Oil on canvas. Private collection.

Self-presentation for a 1915 exhibition
With the development of photography, *static passéist* painting has lost every prerogative. The cinema kills static contemplation. What we see at a film show is a painting in motion which transforms itself to reproduce a given action.

Static passéist painting is finished because it can render only a single facet of the innumerable aspects of nature. Mechanics have overtaken the *passéist painter*, leaving him as the poor imitator of static exterior forms. So we must not stop to contemplate the traditional corpse. The artist must find new energy in creating an art that no machine can imitate and only the Creative Genius of the artist can conceive. Futurism, a predestined force for progress — not fashion — creates a style of directional, synthetic abstract forms suggested by the dynamic forces of the universe.

ART - 1st Period: personal verist objective — rebellion against academic schools — analysis of our lives — solution Divisionist experiments (lights environments — psyche objects people). Struggles labour pleasure — achievements glorious career recognized by public artists critics.

2nd Period — FUTURISM — EVOLUTION: total denial own work + career (...) Continuation research. Definitive abandon analysis reality — Creation new Futurist style: synthetic abstract subjective dynamic forms. Still research + struggle.

FUTURISMO AVANTI...

Oil on canvas, 77 × 77 (30³/₈ × 30³/₈).
Signed lower left: FUTUR BALLA. On the back: DINAMISMO ANDAMENTALE N. 47.
Provenance: Casa Balla.
Exhibitions: Padova, 1983, p. 31; Roma, 1986, no. 4; New York, 1986, no. 38.

Compenetrazione di spazi (*Interpenetration of Spaces*), c. 1919.

The space of artifice

It has become almost a commonplace to talk about Balla's work for a new environment (from furniture to clothing, from lamps to screens, from ceramics to foulards, from frames to lamp-shades). In a note the painter seems to consider this activity as a source of daily bread, but in reality it was much more than that. To think about the environment means leaving the picture, cancelling "art for art's sake", abandoning the nineteenth century Bohemian attic in order to make the future explode in the streets.

This attitude of Balla's took on a quite different importance when it became part of European culture. When Balla, with Depero and Prampolini, went to represent Italy at the Paris Exposition in 1925, the Futurist ideas (almost exhausted for them) became part of the new panorama of Art Déco. In Balla's works of the Twenties there is no neo-Futurism, but rather the deliberate application of this sparkling new harmony.

This painting can be "decorative" precisely because it is abstract, because it is "simple" — in a word, because it is reproduceable. The idea of an art invented by one man but designed to be practised by everybody for everybody is another of the *grandes illusions* that the historic avant-garde left to its degenerate offspring.

The study decorated by Balla in his house in Via Oslavia. Note, above, the sculpture *Linee di forza del pugno di Boccioni* (*Force-lines of Boccioni's Fist*). Photo by Maurizio di Puolo.

Mosaic, 16 × 23.3 (6¹/₄ × 9¹/₈).
Provenance: Casa Balla.

143

Paravento, progetto (Screen design), c. 1915.

Study for *Paravento con linea di velocità (Screen with Line of Speed)*, c. 1915. Watercolour on paper. Private collection.

Front and back part of a *Paravento con Linea di velocità e Vortice (Screen with Line of Speed and Vortex)*, c. 1915. Oil on canvas (fixed to a wooden frame). Private collection.

The descriptions of some eye-witnesses can take us into Balla's brilliantly coloured, lively studio where every shape had been reinvented — a house he had turned into a fantastic atelier.
I. Corpechot (1919): "His studio is a *cabaret physique*... he was wearing a Futurist tie — a green and yellow bow in the shape of an aeroplane — and yellow and white Futurist shoes."
Virgilio Marchi (1928): "Balla was wearing black patent-leather shoes with white laces, trousers in a tiny check pattern, a multi-coloured waistcoat and shirt, a dark jacket cut asymmetrically to a point, with violet lapels, a square stick, and a scent invented by his lady-wife for afternoon and Sunday occasions. [...] Among the crowd in his studio soldiers' uniforms predominated."
Fortunato Depero (1933): "The workshop of my teacher. He was the first to encourage me. Balla has a living room floating on a cliff in the shape of a house [...] thrown out over the tall green flowerbeds of the Villa Borghese gardens."
Francesco Cangiullo: "Kaleidoscopic magic of aggressive colours. Gaudy multi-coloured paper reflected in sheets of tin-foil, celluloid eyes shining tremulously in a picture, fantastic lamps made of yellow and green tissue-paper lit by the sun, Futurist studies of abstract speed. And violet and scarlet lacquers, crystalline enamels, satin, damask. And Balla dizzily animating his pyrotechnical environment, singing, dancing and accompanying himself like a man possessed, his chest crushed under his guitar."

Tempera on paper, 37 × 25.5 (14⁵/₈ × 10).
Signed lower left: BALLA FUTURISTA (stamped with the "Pugno di Boccioni").
Provenance: Casa Balla; Saletta Barbera, Firenze; Saverio Busiri Vici, Roma.
Exhibitions: Roma, 1971-72, no. 025; Paris, 1972, no. 014; Torino, 1974, no. 24; Wien, 1985, no. 24; Zürich, 1985, no. 25; New York, 1986, no. 30.
Bibliography: *Archivi del Futurismo*, 1962, no. 189a (not reproduced); Fagiolo, 1968 (1970, part III), no. 129; Fagiolo, 1972; De Marchis, 1977, no. 80; Lista, 1982, no. 525.

Futur panca (Future Bench), c. 1920.

VISITATE LA
CASA FUTURISTA
DI **BALLA**
OGNI DOMENICA DALLE 15 ALLE 19
VIA NICOLO' PORPORA, 2
ROMA

The announcement published in the paper *Roma futurista* in May 1919.

Painted wood, 69.6 × 65 × 42 ($27^{3}/_{8}$ × $25^{5}/_{8}$ × $16^{1}/_{2}$).
Provenance: Casa Balla.

Paralume (*Lampshade*), c. 1915.
Watercolour on paste-board, 9.8 × 27.5 (3⁷/₈ × 10⁷/₈).
Provenance: Casa Lovatelli Gaetani, Roma; Galleria Emporio Floreale, Roma.
Exhibitions: Roma, 1976, no. 28.

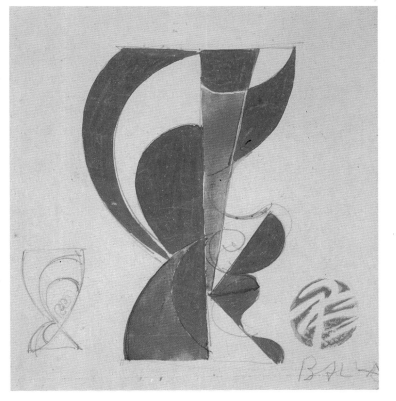

Progetto per vaso di fiori con linea di velocità (*Design for Flower-vase with Line of Speed*), c. 1915.

Pencil and tempera on paper, 20.5 × 19.5 (8 × 7⁵/₈).
Signed lower right: BALLA (stamped with the "Pugno di Boccioni").
Provenance: Casa Balla.
Exhibitions: Torino, 1963, no. 270; Wien, 1985, no. 23; Zürich, 1985, no. 26; New York, 1986, no. 31.
Bibliography: *Archivi del Futurismo*, 1962, no. 169; Lista, 1982, no. 526.

Sedia futurista (*Futurist Chair*), c. 1918.

La seggiola dell'uomo strano (*The Chair of the Strange Man*), c. 1929. Oil on canvas. Private collection.

Futur-reality (*Futur-realtà*) was the title given by Balla to a lively design for objects produced in 1917. But the first reality that Balla aspired to modify was that of his own environment. For his house in Via Paisiello (and then his new home in Via Oslavia) he designed a series of furniture pieces based on green and yellow colours, a chromatic combination we also find in the painting *Numbers in Love* (*Numeri innamorati*). Not very painterly, perhaps, but certainly meaningful (sun and nature) and also modern. Household objects subsequently became an almost magical and spiritual fact for Balla. He is strangely close to de Chirico's "furniture" paintings. In 1929 he produced a hermetic picture entitled *The Chair of the Strange Man* (*La seggiola dell'uomo strano*). The subject is one of the chairs from his set of Futurist furniture, placed in the centre of the canvas beside his "Ego", irradiating thought-forms.

Painted wood, 102.9 × 45.8 × 36.8 (40½ × 17¾ × 14½).
Provenance: Casa Balla.
Exhibitions: Torino, 1963, no. 291; Roma, 1968; Zürich, 1985, no. 28; New York, 1986, no. 33.
Bibliography: Dortch Dorazio, 1970, no. 227; Venezia, 1986, p. 322.

Exhibitions and bibliography quoted in the entries

Exhibitions

Roma, Casa d'Arte Bragaglia, *Giacomo Balla*, presentation by G. Balla, 4-13 October 1918.

Milano, Galleria Centrale d'Arte, Palazzo Cova, *Grande esposizione nazionale futurista - Quadri, complessi plastici, architettura, tavole parolibere, teatro plastico futurista e moda futurista*, March-April 1919.

Venezia, *XV Esposizione internazionale d'arte - Sala futurista*, presentation by E. Prampolini, April-October 1926.

Bologna, Casa del Fascio, *Grande mostra di pittura futurista*, January 1927.

Imola, Ridotto del Teatro Comunale, *Grande mostra d'arte futurista*, 29 January - 10 February 1928.

Venezia, *XVII Esposizione internazionale d'arte*, May-September 1930.

Paris, Galerie 23, *Peintres futuristes italiens*, presentation by G. Severini, 27 December 1929 - 3 January 1930.

Zürich, Kunsthaus, *Futurismo e pittura metafisica*, texts by P. Wehrli and M. Bill, November-December 1950.

Roma, Galleria Origine, *Omaggio a G. Balla futurista*, April 1951.

Roma, Palazzo delle Esposizioni, *VI Quadriennale*, preface by F.T. Marinetti, December 1951 - April 1952.

New York, Rose Fried Gallery, *The Futurists - Balla Severini 1912-1918*, presentations by J. Maritain and L. Venturi, 25 January - 26 February 1954.

New York, Sidney Janis Gallery, *Futurism: Balla Boccioni Carrà Russolo Severini*, 22 March - 1 May 1954.

Paris, Galerie Cahiers d'Art, *Exposition de peintures, de gouaches et de dessins de Giacomo Balla*, presentation by C. Zervos, 12 April - 11 May 1957.

Roma, Palazzo Barberini (then at Winterthur and Münich), *Mostra del futurismo*, entries on Balla by M.L. Drudi Gambillo, Spring-Summer 1959.

Roma, Palazzo delle Esposizioni, *VIII Quadriennale*, presentation by E. Francia, December 1959 - April 1960.

Venezia, XXX Biennale, *Mostra storica del futurismo*, presentation by G. Ballo, June-October 1960.

Torino, Galleria Civica d'Arte Moderna, *Giacomo Balla*, organized by E. Crispolti and M.L. Drudi Gambillo, 4 April 1963.

Hamburg, Kunstverein in Hamburg, *Italien 1905-1025 - Futurismus und Pittura metafisica*, 28 September - 3 November 1963 (then, Frankfurt, Frankfurter Kunstverein, Kuratorium Kulturelles Frankfurt, Steinernes Haus Römerberg, 16 November 1963 - 5 January 1964).

Torino, Galleria Notizie, *Giacomo Balla*, March 1967.

Firenze, Palazzo Strozzi, *Arte moderna in Italia*, organized by C.L. Ragghianti, 26 February - 28 May 1967.

Roma, Galleria dell'Obelisco, *Giacomo Balla: Balla prefuturista - Luce e movimento - Gli stati d'animo, Ricostruzione futurista dell'universo*, with three monographs by M. Fagiolo (subsequently in vol. II, 1970), February-June 1968; no numbers in catalogues.

Venezia, XXXIV Biennale, *Quattro maestri del futurismo italiano*, organized by M. Calvesi, July-September 1968.

Roma, Studio d'Arte Moderna Margutta, *Balla - I Centenario della nascita*, 22 March - 14 April 1971.

Roma, Galleria Nazionale d'Arte Moderna, *Giacomo Balla (1871-1958)*, organized by G. de Marchis, G. Piantoni, B. Sani, 24 May - 2 July 1972.

Newcastle, Hatton Gallery, University of Newcastle, *Exhibition of Italian Futurism 1909-1919*, 4 November - 9 December 1972 (then Edinburgh, Royal Scottish Academy, 17 December 1972 - 14 January 1973).

Paris, Musée National d'Art Moderne, *Le futurisme 1906-16*, organized by G. Ballo, F. Cachin-Nora, J. Leymarie, F. Russoli, 19 September - 19 November 1973.

Düsseldorf, Stadtische Kunsthalle, *Futurismus 1909-17*, texts by F. Russoli, M. Calvesi, F.W. Heckmanns, 25 March - 28 April 1974.

Torino, Galleria Martano, *Balla*, organized by M. Fagiolo, May 1974.

Roma, Emporio Floreale, *34 paralumi di Giacomo Balla*, presentation by M. Calvesi, December 1976 - January 1977.

Verona, Museo di Castelvecchio, *Giacomo Balla - Studi ricerche oggetti*, organized by L. Marcucci, February-March 1976.

Modena, Galleria Fonte d'Abisso, *Giacomo Balla - Tipologie di astrazione, opere dal 1912 al 1930*, organized by M. Fagiolo and L. Marcucci, 15 March - 15 May 1980.

Torino, Mole Antonelliana, *Ricostruzione futurista dell'universo*, organized by E. Crispolti, June-October, 1980.

Milano, Galleria Daverio, *Selezione 5 - Pittura italiana e arti decorative 1910-1940*, 27 November-December 1980.

Basel, Art 82, *Futur-Balla un profeta dell'avanguardia*, organized by P. Sprovieri and M. Fagiolo, 1982.

Padova, Galleria Civica, *Giacomo Balla*, 1983.

New York, Art for Architecture Gallery, *Futurism - Selected Works and Documents*, organized by M. Fagiolo, May 1984.

New York, *Futur-Balla - Studi e disegni*, organized by M. Fagiolo, 1985.

Wien, Galerie Würthle, *Giacomo Balla - Arbeiten von 1912 bis 1928*, 4-26 June 1985.

Zurich, Turscke & Turscke Galerie, *Giacomo Balla - Werke von 1912 bis 1928*, 5 October - 16 November 1985.

Roma, Galleria Sprovieri, *Arte astratta italiana*, organized by M. Fagiolo, February-March 1986.

New York, Kouros Gallery, *Works by Giacomo Balla from 1905 to 1928*, organized by P. Sprovieri and M. Fagiolo, 15 March - 24 April 1986.

Venezia, Palazzo Grassi, *Futurismo & Futurismi*, organized by Pontus Hulten, May-September 1986.

Venezia, Studio d'Arte Barnabò, *Esposizione di pittura futurista*, organized by M. Fagiolo, July-September 1986 (then Roma, Galleria Sprovieri, October-November 1986).

Vancouver, Art Gallery, *Futur-Balla*, organized by M. Fagiolo, 12 August - 13 October 1986.

Bibliography

V. Costantini, *Pittura italiana contemporanea*, Milano, 1934.

C. Zervos (ed.), "Un demi-siècle d'art italien", in *Cahiers d'Art*, no. 1, 1950.

Archivi del Futurismo, ed. M.L. Drudi Gambillo and T. Fiori, De Luca, Roma, 1962, vol. II.

E. Crispolti, "Introduzione", in W. Hofmann, *La scultura del XX secolo*, Cappelli, Bologna, 1962.

G. Ballo, *La linea dell'arte italiana dal simbolismo alle opere moltiplicate*, Mediterranee, Roma, 1964.

A. Barricelli, *Balla*, De Luca, Roma, 1967.

M. Calvesi, "Penetrazione e magia nell'arte di Balla", in *L'arte moderna*, Fabbri, Milano, 1967-68, vol. V.

M. Fagiolo, *Balla prefuturista - Le compenetrazioni iridescenti - Ricostruzione futurista dell'universo*, 3 monographs, Bulzoni, Roma, 1968 (then updated, in *Futur-Balla*, Roma, 1970).

V. Dortch Dorazio, *Balla - An Album of His Life and Works*, Alfieri, Venezia / Wittenborn, New York, 1970.

M. Martin, *Futurist Art and Theory, 1909-1915*, Clarendon Press, Oxford, 1968.

M. Fagiolo, "The Futurist Construction of the Universe", in *Italy - The New Domestic Landscape*, The Museum of Modern Art, New York / Centro Di, Firenze, 1972, pp. 293-301.

G. de Marchis, *Balla, l'aura futurista*, Einaudi, Torino, 1972.

C. Block, *Geschichte der Abstrakten Kunst*, Köln, 1975.

G. Lista, *Giacomo Balla*, Modena, 1982 (documentation by the Galleria Fonte D'Abisso: G. Battaglia, A. Gambuzzi, S. Poggianella).

G. Lista, *Giacomo Balla futuriste*, L'Age d'Homme, Lausanne, 1984.

Bibliographical guide

Archivi del Futurismo, ed. M.L. Drudi Gambillo, T. Fiori, De Luca, Roma, 1959 (texts), 1962 (catalogue).
This is the first work on Balla, now obsolete (a reprint exists: De Luca-Mondadori, Milano, 1986).

J.C. Taylor, *Futurism*, The Museum of Modern Art, New York, 1961.
The first work on Balla and his time, in the country to which we owe the real rediscovery of Futurism.

Giacomo Balla, catalogue of the exhibition, ed. E. Crispolti and M.L. Drudi Gambillo, Museo Civico, Torino, 1963.
A work which is still fundamental today, and an incomparable exhibition.

M. Fagiolo, *Omaggio a Balla*, Bulzoni, Roma, 1967.
Reopens the discussion on Balla.

M. Calvesi, *Penetrazione e magia nell'arte di Giacomo Balla*, in *L'arte moderna*, vol. V, Fabbri, Milano, 1967-68.
A very penetrating historical and critical analysis.

M. Fagiolo, *Balla pre-futurista - Le compenetrazioni iridescenti, Ricostruzione futurista dell'universo*, Bulzoni, Roma, 1968 (2nd edition with appendix, 1970).
An analysis of three specific moments of Balla's work, with unpublished documents.

V. Dortch Dorazio, *Balla - An Album of His Life and Work*, Alfieri, Venezia-Wittenborn, New York, 1970.
A useful comparison between photography and painting in a good short biography.

Giacomo Balla, ed. G. De Marchis, L. Velani, B. Sani, Galleria Nazionale d'Arte Moderna, Roma, 1971 (with variants, Paris, 1972).
An arguable critical approach. The catalogue is

important for L. Velani's regest.

G. Lista, *Giacomo Balla*, Modena, 1982.
Album of the photographs owned by the family, decidedly uneven critical text. Introduction added. By the same author there is a second volume (ed. L'Age de l'Homme, Lausanne) where a number of forgeries appear for the first time.

M. Fagiolo, *Balla, profeta dell'avanguardia*, Basel, 1982.
Biography with new documents.

I taccuini di Balla (Nos. 4, 3, 5), published as a re-print with commentary by M. Fagiolo, Martano, Torino, 1982-86.

Futurismo & Futurismi, ed. Pontus Hulten, Bompiani, Milano, 1986 (an English language edition exists under the same title).
The first impression is of huge, useless effort, but the book is in fact useful for popularizing the subject internationally.

DATE DUE

	WITHDRAWN